The Businesses of Sampford Peverell

Volume 1: Shops

by Allan Weller, Christine Mason,
Heather Culpin, Jeff Parsons and Peter Bowers

GW00643262

A Sampford Peverell Society publication

Dedicated to the memory of
Christine Mason

Previous publications by the Sampford Peverell Society

Sampford Peverell during the First World War, by Peter Bowers, Clive Cotton, Heather Culpin and Allan Weller, published by the Sampford Peverell Society, 2018

The Schools of Sampford Peverell, by Carole Bond, Christopher Chesney, Christine Mason, Jacky McKechnie, Jenny Parsons, Peter Bowers and Vivienne Heeley, published by the Sampford Peverell Society, 2015

A Village Childhood by Denis Cluett, edited by the Sampford Peverell Society and published by Charles Scott-Fox, 2007

Sampford Peverell: The Village, Church, Chapels and Rectories, Editor and publisher Charles Scott-Fox, 2007

Printed by Hedgerow Print Ltd

Published by the Sampford Peverell Society 2020

ISBN: 978-0-9933171-2-5

Contents

Introduction and Acknowledgements   i
Glossary   iii
Graph of the number of shops   vi
Maps showing the location of shops   vii
Chapter 1 - Early shops   1
Chapter 2 – Bakers   9
    Introduction   9
    18 Higher Town – The Ghost House Bakery   10
    Other Bakers   20
    4 Higher Town - Southwood's Bakery   20
    14 Higher Town - Grocer's shop   22
    6 Chains Road – Bennett's Bakery   23
    Lower Town - Coles' Bakery   25
    Higher Town and Mount Pleasant - Taylor's Bakery   25
Chapter 3 – Butchers   27
    Introduction   27
    12 Lower Town – Challis   28
    Quay Head, Boobery and 9 Higher Town – Paulett House   37
    Other Butchers   41
Chapter 4 - Grocers and Drapers   49
    Introduction   49
    9 Higher Town – Chorleys   50
    11a Higher Town - Halls   56
    14 Higher Town - Cowlins   60
    21 Higher Town – London House   69
    24 Higher Town – Coombe Cottage   74
    25 and 27 Lower Town – Barum House   76
    8, 10 and 12 Lower Town – the 'Challis' buildings   88
Chapter 5 – Newsagents   101
    Introduction   101
    27 Lower Town - Barum House, 1914 - 1933   102

11 Higher Town - Rose Cottage, 1933 – late 1950s   103
27 Lower Town - Barum House, late 1950s - 1999   104
21 Higher Town - London House, 1999 - 2010   105
3a The Mews, Smithys Way - SPAR shop, 2010 - today   106

Chapter 6 - The Post Office   **107**
Introduction   107
10 Lower Town – 1851 – 1881   108
2 Lower Town – Bridge House 1881 – 1913   110
21 Higher Town - London House 1913 – 1917   112
2 Lower Town – Bridge House 1917 - 1951   114
8 Lower Town – Challis Stores 1951 – c1963   115
21 Higher Town - London House c1963 – 2010   117
3a The Mews, Smithys Way, SPAR shop 2010 onwards   120

Chapter 7 - Shoes   **123**
Introduction   123
17th century Sampford Peverell shoemakers   125
18th century Sampford Peverell shoemakers   125
The Darch family   126
Other shoemakers   129

Chapter 8 - Tailors   **137**
Introduction   137
17th and 18th century tailors   138
19th century tailors and the Taylor family   140
20th century tailors   144

Chapter 9 - Shops in 2020   **147**
Little Turberfield Farm Shop – Station Road   147
SPAR shop, 3a The Mews, Smithys Way   150

Notes   **153**
Appendix 1: The 1852 Petition   **155**
Appendix 2: Examples of Mr Thomas's Advertisements   **156**
Sources and Bibliography   **159**
Maps of the local area   **160**
Index of Surnames and Addresses   **163**

Introduction

This is the first in a series of books by the Sampford Peverell Society about the businesses in the village. Further volumes will follow, covering pubs, hostelries, services, craft-workers and heavy industries. In this volume about the shops the reader can discover just how the retail industry of Sampford Peverell has changed over the last two hundred years, mirroring what has occurred in many other villages around the country. We have restricted the scope of this volume to just those businesses listed in the Contents; other businesses will be included in later volumes.

Readers may wonder whether 'shops' were a significant feature of the village's history, given that only two remain today. For centuries, residents of the parish could buy everything that they needed in the village, whether food, clothes or household objects. The number of shops was in double figures throughout the nineteenth century, peaking at eighteen in 1891, and this was despite a gradual drop in population. In the twentieth century the number of shops gradually reduced, due to such factors as easier access to nearby towns, the advent of cars and buses, the greater range of cheaper mass-produced goods available in those towns, and the lure of supermarkets and department stores. From the 1950s the population rose steadily but the number of shops started to plummet, as is evident from the graph on page vi.

The research for this series of publications was carried out business by business, and drew upon a wide range of sources. For the early history, most has been gleaned from old documents and parish records; from the nineteenth century, additional material is available from published directories and newspaper articles which tell fascinating stories of theft, bankruptcy and murder; and into more recent times, personal memories have been provided by recent and current residents of Sampford Peverell.

Although the reader may note that most of the shopkeepers were listed as men, this is largely because women only appeared in the records if they were single or widowed. Generally, married women did not own anything - a business had to be in the husband's name. If a man was married it is very likely that his wife would work with him in the business; very often, a widow would continue to run the business after the death of her husband.

In keeping with our previous practice, the research has been carried out by a team of volunteers, with each member of the team then proceeding to write up their chosen topics. Next, the drafts were swapped between the team members and then reviewed by the whole team, with amendments being suggested and agreed along the way.

The team members for this book were Peter Bowers, Heather Culpin, Christine Mason, Jeff Parsons and Allan Weller. It was very sad that Christine passed away in 2018, before this volume was ready for publication.

Acknowledgements

We have acknowledged some of the contributors to this book in the text and in the captions to photos and illustrations by local artists, but there have been many others, un-named, who have provided some form of assistance e.g. by allowing us to use pictures from their postcard collections, providing photos of their possessions, providing odd 'snippets' of information, and giving us access to the collection of old Sampford Peverell Parish magazines. We thank you all, because without these acts of generosity, the content would have been far less comprehensive.

Peter Bowers, Chairman, Sampford Peverell Society

Glossary

Censuses. Introduced in 1801, censuses of the population of England, Wales and Scotland have been carried out at ten yearly intervals since then, except in 1941. The purpose is to create a statistical record, initially just by occupation and sex within each parish, but from 1841 details of personal names and relationships were recorded, with further information being added in more recent censuses. At the time of writing, those records in the public domain are from 1801 to 1911.

Currency. The pre-decimal currency, used in Great Britain until 1971, was based on the monetary unit of one pound (£1), which comprised 20 shillings (20s), with one shilling equal to 12 pence (12d). Other coinage included a half-crown (2 shillings and 6 pence, written as 2/6d) a florin (2s), a sixpence (6d), a three-penny piece (3d), a half-penny (½d) and a farthing (¼d). To compare values of commodities in the 19th and 20th centuries with what they are today, a useful measure is that of agricultural wages. The average wage of an agricultural labourer in 1850 was 9 shillings per week rising to 16 shillings per week by 1914 (British Labour Statistics – Dept. Employment and Productivity 1971).

Electoral Rolls. Lists of people qualified to vote, together with their place of abode and the name of the property which gave rise to the entitlement, were produced from 1832. This system replaced an earlier system of freeholders' lists, which contained less information. Initially, only a small minority of the more wealthy male inhabitants of a parish were entitled to vote, but subsequent Reform Acts increased the number of electors, until 1928 when the criteria were broadened to all men and women over 21. The voting age was reduced to 18 in 1971. Records survive for Sampford Peverell for most years from 1833 onwards.

Journeyman. Trade and craft workers such as shoemakers and tailors went through three stages of employment. A novice would learn their trade as an apprentice, in many cases living with the family of the 'master' from whom they were learning. An apprenticeship would usually last seven or more years. Once qualified they became a 'journeyman', which meant they were paid on a daily basis and often worked away from home. Eventually they might be able to set up business for themselves as a 'master' of their trade.

Land Tax records. Land Tax was introduced in 1692 as a means of raising government revenue. The records show owners and occupiers of properties within a parish, together with the amount of tax assessed. Records for Sampford Peverell survive for most years from 1744 to 1936, except for the period from 1832 to 1861.

Land Valuation Survey, 1910. A survey of land carried out to determine land ownership and valuation was undertaken for taxation purposes between 1910 and 1915. It is sometimes referred to as the Lloyd George survey. Details of each property in the country were recorded in field books. There are four field books which cover Sampford Peverell, and they are held in the National Archives. The details include owners, occupiers, number of rooms, outbuildings, and occasionally hand-drawn plans of farms.

Map of the Manor, 1796. A map of the parish of Sampford Peverell was surveyed on behalf of the Right Honorable Earl Poulett, who owned the manor at that time. Drawn to a large scale, it is the earliest map of the parish that is available.

St Boniface Home for Waifs and Strays. The Church of England Society for Waifs and Strays set up a home for boys in Lower Town in 1907 in the former premises of the East Devon County School. There, about 60 boys, who came from broken homes or were orphaned, were accommodated and cared for until they reached at least 14 years of age. The Home closed in 1952.

Tithe Map and Apportionments. The Tithe Commutation Act of 1836 was an Act to replace the ancient system of payment of a 'tithe' (i.e. one tenth) in kind with monetary payments. In order to do so, all the land in England and Wales was mapped to show for each numbered plot the ownership, tenancy, type and value, with the information about each numbered plot being published as the 'apportionments'. The map and apportionments survive for Sampford Peverell, where the survey was carried out in 1844.

The 1852 Petition. This Petition was signed by many of the businessmen in the parish. For further details, see Appendix 1.

The 1939 Register. This Register was compiled as the result of the National Registration Act in September 1939, at the start of the Second World War. Enumerators visited every household in Britain, gathering names, addresses, birth dates, occupations and so on. The information was used to issue identity cards and ration books. The data can be searched in www.findmypast.co.uk and ancestry.co.uk.

Trade Directories. Directories were produced from the 18th century onwards to identify prominent inhabitants and tradespeople within specific towns, cities and counties. Information about Sampford Peverell was first published in White's Directory of Devon in 1850. Thereafter, several other publishers produced directories for Devon, at various intervals up to the Second World War. There was also a local directory for Tiverton and District, usually listing just the head of each household together with their occupation and approximate address, which was published by Gregory, Son and Tozer, at sundry dates between 1894 and 1926.

Weights and measures. From 1825 until 1973, when the United Kingdom joined the European Economic Community, the system of weights and measures used throughout the country was based on Imperial units. Since 1973, metric weights and measures have been gradually introduced, although vestiges of the Imperial system still remain in use today. For weights, 16 ounces (oz) were equal to one pound (lb), the latter being equivalent to about 0.45 kilograms. 112 pounds (lbs) were equal to 1 hundred weight (cwt). For liquid measures, eight pints were equal to one gallon, which is approximately 4.5 litres. For lengths, 12 inches were equal to one foot, three feet made one yard, and 1760 yards were the same as one mile, which is equivalent to about 1.6 kilometres. For areas, one acre is equal to approximately 0.4 hectares.

Links to family trees.
In conducting the research for this book, it was necessary to construct family trees for a number of individuals. Subscribers to ancestry.co.uk can see family trees of some of the families referred to in this book at http://www.sampevsoc.co.uk/family-trees.html

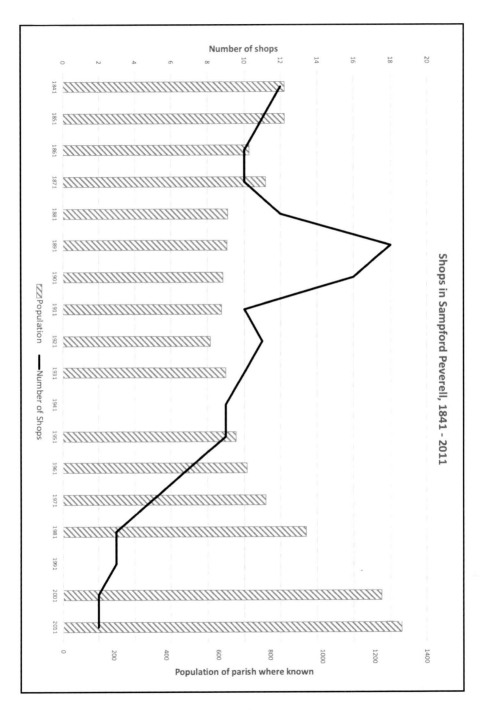

Shops in Sampford Peverell, 1841 - 2011

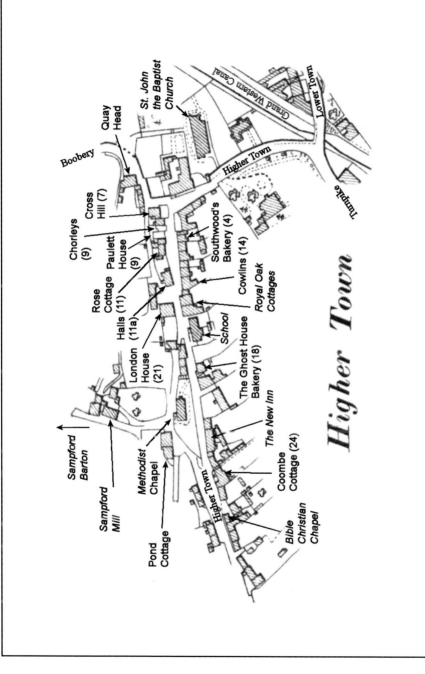

Higher Town

Map based on 1904 Ordnance Survey, prepared by Richard Horrocks

Shops in Higher Town, Sampford Peverell

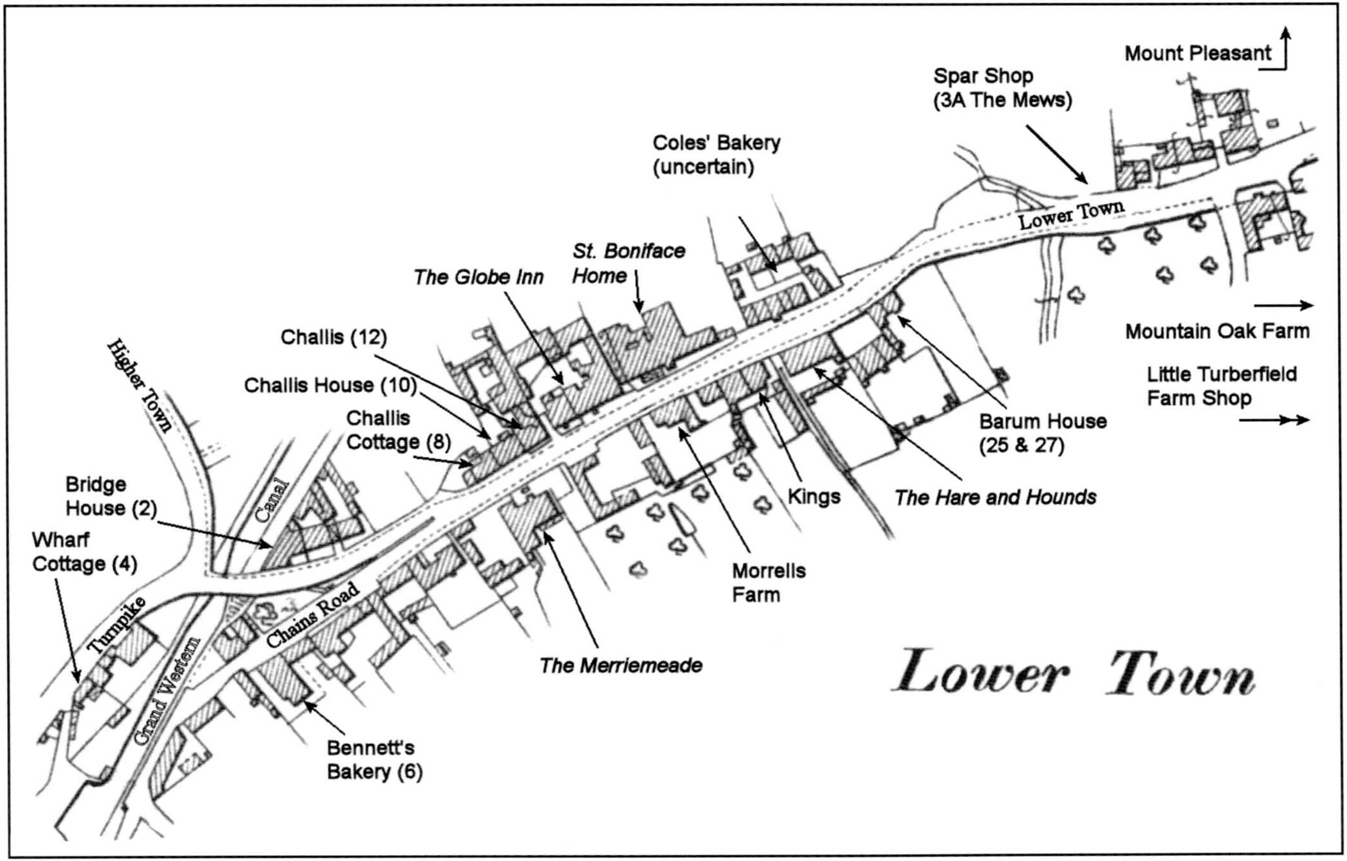

Mount Pleasant
Spar Shop
(3A The Mews)
Coles' Bakery
(uncertain)
Lower Town
St. Boniface
Home
The Globe Inn
Challis (12)
Challis House (10)
Challis
Cottage (8)
Higher Town
Canal
Bridge
House (2)
Wharf
Cottage (4)
Turnpike
Grand Western
Chains Road
Bennett's
Bakery (6)
The Merriemeade
Morrells
Farm
Kings
The Hare and Hounds
Barum House
(25 & 27)
Mountain Oak Farm
Little Turberfield
Farm Shop
Lower Town

Shops in Lower Town, Sampford Peverell

Map based on 1904 Ordnance Survey, prepared by Richard Horrocks

Chapter 1

Early shops

When we think of a shop today, we imagine a building which is open to the public at set times and from which are sold a selection of goods sourced from a variety of suppliers and manufacturers, often from around the world. Of course, shops have not always been like this, but have evolved to this state over hundreds of years. In this book we will examine the evidence for the evolution of shops in the village of Sampford Peverell and attempt to document their development and decline.

Whilst markets probably provided the means by which local produce was exchanged and sold ever since the settlement became established, there is no evidence to support the existence of one in Sampford Peverell until 1220. The weekly market would have originally been held on a Sunday, to take advantage of the increased trade from the regular gathering of people for Church services. Sunday was also the only non-working day of the week for most people. In, or shortly before, 1220, it would appear that the Lord of the Manor, Hugh Peverell, altered the market day from Sunday to Saturday. The probable reason for him to have done so was pressure from the Church, whose clergymen were concerned about the unruly behaviour that generally accompanied markets, disrupting the Lord's Day, and keeping people from attending their Church services.

A medieval market   *Illustration by Val Weller*

Over a hundred years later, in 1335, Sampford's Saturday market was finally given royal assent in a Charter granted by King Edward III to Elias de Cotelye. Elias' wife Margery had inherited the Manor of Sampford Peverell in 1300 after her brother, Sir Thomas Peverell, the owner, died at the young age of 22.

1633 Market Charter   Somerset Heritage Centre DD/PT/S1742/2

The weekly-held Saturday market continued until 1633, when the then Lord of the Manor, John, Lord Paulett, Baron of Hinton St George, obtained a Charter from King Charles I for the market day to be changed to Friday. The lavishly illuminated Charter document is now kept at the Somerset Heritage Centre, and is reproduced above.

Many lords founded boroughs on their estates by the simple process of staking out plots and inviting settlers, in the hope that a commercial centre would grow up from which they could collect a toll. In this way, some of the village properties could be held under burgage tenure, which involved personal freedom, a small money rent and liberty to sell the property (known as a 'burgage plot') while other properties could remain part of the manor, to ensure that the lord's land would continue to be productive. After 1378 there are several documents showing that some of the houses in the village were designated as coming under 'the Borough' and others as under 'the Manor', right up until the time when the Manor was sold off piecemeal, between 1805 and 1810.

17th c. document headings

Typically, burgage plots were acquired by craftsmen and shopkeepers who would sell their wares from the fronts of their houses. Burgage plots were set out such that each had a narrow road frontage, but with a very considerable depth, where workshops could be situated as well as leaving space for growing vegetables and keeping animals. The size of burgage plots varied from one borough to another. Narrow burgage plots enabled prospective customers to examine the wares of several craftsmen and shopkeepers without having to walk very far up or down the street, and also provided the lord with the greatest possible number of plots with desirable road

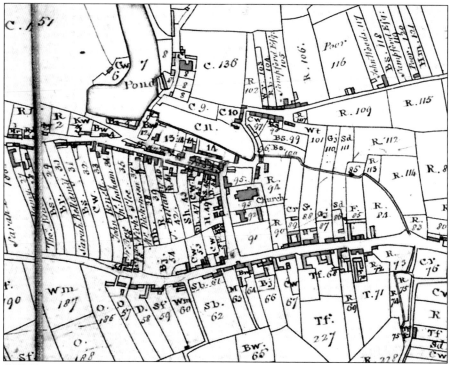

1796 Manorial Map showing burgage plots in Higher Town and Boobery   *Devon Heritage Centre*
1044B/M/E/90

frontages in the space available. The more craftsmen that the lord could attract to his borough, the better were the prospects for the local economy, which in turn would provide property rents and market tolls and taxes for the lord.

In Sampford Peverell, the original layout of burgage plots can still be observed in a few of the older properties in Higher Town and Boobery. They are even more apparent on the 1796 Manorial map, before more recent changes were made to land holdings. Measurements for one of the remaining burgage plots in Boobery, the boundaries of which are unlikely to have changed, were found to be 2 perches by 28 perches (the standard measure for land at that time was the perch, with one perch being 5.5 yards), thereby enclosing an area of about one third of an acre.

The first mention of a shop occurs in a 1391 grant of a burgage plot from Joan Riche, widow of William Riche, to her daughter and son-in-law, translated from Latin as follows:

> Burgage in Sampford Peverell between [the] land of Roger Metton called Wynhay on [the] West; burgage of Alice relative of Wm. Smyth on [the] East and a shop which William Riche acquired by gift of Oliver Dynham Junior, which lies between the burgage of John Chapman on the East and the place of fish shops [or stalls] on the West in the high street of Sampford Peverell.

A late medieval shop   *Illustration by Val Weller*

In this document, the 'high street' is believed to refer to Higher Town, although we can only speculate as to the precise whereabouts of William Riche's shop and the place of the fish stalls.

Fairs were also important to the commercial life of the village. Typically, fairs attracted buyers from far and wide as well as itinerant traders selling hides, skins, wool, metals, ironmongery and cloth. People would drive their surplus livestock to the fair in the hope of getting the best price. Also travelling the fair circuit would be musicians and entertainers: for local people, it was a time for 'letting their hair down', often with much feasting and drinking. In order for a settlement to hold a fair on a certain Church festival or Saint's day, the lord of the manor had to be granted royal assent. Sampford Peverell was granted its first fair by King Edward III in 1335, to take place on the festival of the Annunciation, which falls on 25th March, Lady Day, traditionally the day in the year upon which labourers were hired.

Nothing more is known about the Annunciation Day fair. Perhaps it was unsuccessful, because in 1487 an application was made by Lady Margaret Beaufort, who then owned the manor of Sampford Peverell, for two more

Sampford Fair Day, Lower Town, circa 1900

fairs. She made the application to her son, King Henry VII, who granted her request for the following:

- A fair on Saint Alphege's day, the 19th April. The new fair was to be held on the Saint's day itself and two days on each side.

- A fair on the feast day of the Decollation (i.e. beheading) of St John the Baptist, which falls on 29th August. This was also a five day fair.

Of these two annual fairs, the one held in April continued to be held right up until about 1950, becoming one of the main cattle fairs in the area. Little is known of the other fair, which probably died out in the early 19th century.

Very few records, which might shed light on the existence of shops, survive from before the 17th century. From the early 1600s there are a small number of property leases, some of which provide names together with occupations. For example, John and Thomas Saunders were cordwainers (i.e. shoe-makers) in 1608, but whether they had shops which were separate from their dwellings is unlikely, as there is no mention of them in these leases. It is not until the middle of the 17th century that we find another reference to a shop. In Hugh Pullen's will of 1658 he bequeathed to his daughter Joan 'all the goods which she hath in the shopp of mine' - without any indication of the type of goods or the location of the shop. During the 1660s there was a dire shortage of small denomination coinage, to the extent that it adversely affected shopkeepers' trade. In many towns around the country privately made tokens were produced by traders for values such as ¼d, ½d and 1d, to make up for the government's failure

John Stone's half-penny, 1670

to provide them. In Sampford Peverell, John Stone, who we believe was a mercer (i.e. dealer in cloth and other commodities) produced some ½d tokens in 1670. Perhaps they were used in Pullens' shop.

Even as we move into the 18th century, there is no further mention of shops, except in the context of workshops (e.g. a blacksmith's shop), and butchers (who may or may not have had shops). From the middle of the 18th century comes the first record of a person whose occupation was a shopkeeper: in 1750 John Ballamy, shop-keeper, married Sarah Cowling by licence. Unfortunately, we cannot tell where John Ballamy's shop was, because the Land Tax records show that he was the occupier of more than one property in the parish.

During the second half of the 18th century shops were becoming an established feature of the village. From Trewman's Exeter Flying Post newspaper report of 5th September 1777 comes a disturbing report, as follows:

> Last week a melancholy accident happened at Sandord (sic) Peverell. A poor man, his wife, and child, who had been troubled with the Itch, applied to a shop-keeper for some cream of tartar, who, instead of the thing required, through mistake, supplied them with arsenic; in consequence of which the man and child died the next day, but it is hoped that the woman will recover.

Although no names are mentioned in the report, Joseph Clarke and three-year-old Mary Clarke were the likely casualties, whose burial records are to be found on 29 August 1777 in the registers of the parish church. Who the careless shop-keeper was remains a mystery.

From the early part of the 19th century, it becomes evident that there were shops in both Higher Town and Lower Town. One surprising, but useful, source for names and occupations from this period is bankruptcy records. A spate of bankruptcies followed an economic depression which started in 1814, caused by land speculation and price inflation during the Napoleonic Wars (Ivy Pinchbeck, p68, see Bibliography). One such economic casualty was John Shuckburgh who was declared bankrupt in 1815. He had formerly been living in Sampford Peverell, but his extravagant lifestyle had caught up with him and he was now incarcerated in the debtors' prison in Exeter. Amongst the list of 50 people in Devon and Bristol to whom he was indebted were the following retailers from Sampford Peverell : James Surridge, butcher; Mary Skinner, baker; John Curwood, shop-keeper; and William Hellier, shop-keeper. The fact that John Shuckburgh had managed to run up so many bills with traders, ranging from clothing to wines and from furniture to groceries, is evidence of the way that business was transacted at the time. Shuckburgh's bankruptcy may have proved the final straw for shop-keeper John Curwood junior, one of Shuckburgh's creditors, who himself was declared bankrupt in the following year.

Chapter 2

Bakers

Introduction

Cereals are highly nutritious, containing the protein, carbohydrate and many of the vitamins needed for a healthy diet and humans have been consuming them in the form of bread for ten thousand years. In medieval England bread was made from various cereals, such as rye, barley, oats or wheat, or a combination of them. Wheat could only be grown on enriched soil, and so was the preserve of the better off. As animal husbandry

A bakery   *Child Land by Pietsch and Rictor on www.gutenberg.org*

became more widespread to satisfy a growing market for meat, so too did the availability of dung for enriching the soil, and eventually wheat became the dominant flour for making bread. A few households would have had a stone or clay oven in an outhouse, but for most people, bread would have had to be baked by the village baker.

From the Tudor period onwards, the gentry began to install into their houses the sought-after technology of the day: a chimney. Very often, in the inglenook of the chimney, there was a built-in bread oven, so that bread could be baked each day for the household. A few of the older houses in the village today still retain a remnant of their original bread oven, even if it may no longer be in use. Over the 17th and 18th centuries such facilities were also built into the homes of some of the less wealthy, but the peasantry had to make do with a small hearth and no bread oven in their meagre dwellings. Consequently, they were dependent for their bread upon bakers and the local bakehouse.

Early records for bakeries in Sampford Peverell are sparse, but one source indicates that the business of baking could be combined with another that also needed heat: a smithy. A survey of properties in the Manor dating from the early years of the 18th century tells us that 'one cottage with a Smith's Shopp and little bakehouse' was leased to the Banfild (otherwise Banfield) family.

However, it is not until the 19th century that records are sufficiently detailed to provide a narrative about the bakers in the village. Some of the buildings in which they carried on their trade are either unknown or no longer exist, but we will start by focussing on one bakery in Higher Town, which carried on for nearly one hundred years and was the last one in the village to close.

18 Higher Town – The Ghost House Bakery

On the south side of Higher Town, next to where Sampford Peverell Primary School is now situated, there once stood an ancient building, said to have dated from the 16th century. In 1796 it was owned and occupied by Thomas Ballamy, who seems to have inherited it from a relative, William Ballamy of Tiverton, who had died in the previous year. Respected in the community, Thomas Ballamy was also reputed to 'have indulged in smuggling activities and dug a deep hole under the floor of his main sitting room to hide his booty'. Mr Ballamy died in 1801, and the property then passed into the ownership of his son-in-law William Tally.

In 1810, William Tally let the premises to John Chave whose business was that of a 'huckster' or shop-keeper selling a variety of small goods. Not long after Mr Chave took over the premises a series of mysterious happenings took place, which became a topic of national interest, reported in newspapers all over the country as the 'Sampford Ghost'. (*It is intended that this will be the subject of a future book by The Sampford Peverell Society*). Mr Chave moved out of the house two years later, but the story lived on in the minds of the local people, to whom the property, previously known as "Late William Ballamy's" (or simply "Ballamys") became "The Ghost House".

Stories about The Ghost House's past must have been known to George Collins when he bought it from Robert Moore Perkins, a Tiverton schoolmaster, in 1868. George had previously been working as a baker at Southwood's bakery (No. 4 Higher Town) and he acquired the Ghost House

The Ghost House circa 1860   *Courtesy of Devon Archives & Local Studies, WCSL P&D06616*

in order to establish his own bakery there. At that time, it was divided into four separate dwellings, with five tenant families and, as far as we can tell, no part of it was in use as a shop. Indeed, there is no record of a shop having operated there since John Chave's time.

At the time of the census in 1871 George was described as a Master Baker employing two young men, Frederick Heywood aged 18 and Henry Wood aged 20. George was 39, his wife Maria, née Perry, 32 and they had three young children. Unfortunately George Collins died of tuberculosis in 1873 leaving his wife and their children Mary, George and Amy, aged 7, 5 and 3 respectively.

In his will George bequeathed his property to Robert Burroughs, Yeoman, as trustee with all rents going to his widow and upon her death Burroughs was empowered to sell up and divide the proceeds between the children in equal shares. But Maria Collins did not rent out the property initially; instead, she continued to live there and carry on the business as well as she could with three young children.

By 1876 Maria was being courted by 21-year-old Richard Luxon, 14 years her junior. He had been born in Topsham, the son of a fisherman. In the 1871 census his occupation was described as 'General Work Boy' but now he was a baker, like Maria. Where he learnt his trade, or how he improved his position in society so rapidly, is not known. On 4th December 1876 a Marriage Settlement was drawn up between Maria Collins and Richard Luxon, showing the extent of the property she owned. Her main asset was The Ghost House, which consisted of 4 bedrooms, staircase, parlour, sitting room, shop, bakehouse, kitchen and yard. She also had

2 shares in the East Devon County School Association Ltd., indicating that her son George was probably being educated at this private boys' school in the village. They married the next day.

The bakery was now run by Richard Luxon, as is evident from entries in local directories, but he soon got into financial difficulties. In 1880, at a meeting of his creditors in Exeter, it was agreed that he could settle his debts at 5s in the £1 and he was discharged from bankruptcy.

Sacks of flour being delivered to the Ghost House bakery circa 1920

According to the notice of his discharge, he was a baker, grocer and draper, so perhaps he had tried to diversify when times were getting hard.

After this set-back, Richard Luxon managed to continue in business at the Ghost House bakery. In the 1881 census Richard and Maria were recorded as still carrying on the bakery with the assistance of Maria's eldest child Mary Collins. The remainder of the family present comprised her son George by her first marriage, who was still at school, and Sydney, aged 3, a son from the second marriage. However, further problems lay ahead for Richard, as reported in the North Devon Journal of 19 October 1882. He was summonsed and found guilty of selling bread illegally, by not having scales and weights with him when he delivered bread. He was fined £1 with costs.

During the 1880s Richard and Maria went their separate ways, and by 1887 William Conde Thomas had taken over the bakery business at the Ghost House. Maria moved to Lion's Halt, Exeter, where she soon found herself in need of more money. She was able to borrow £95 from John Carter, a baker in Exeter, on the strength of being the beneficial owner of the bakery in Sampford Peverell. She probably needed the money to set up her new bakery business in Exeter, trading under the name of "M Collins", but this venture was short-lived and soon went into receivership. In 1889 her financial affairs were examined by the Official Receiver in Exeter, and a resolution with her creditors was to be sought. The outcome is not stated in the report in the Western Times of 9 October 1889, but she died in the following year.

By 1890 Richard Luxon had moved to Tottenham in London. In the census of the following year he can be found living and working at 12 High Street, Tottenham as a foreman baker, working for Alfred Wood the baker, who was born in Sampford Peverell, the son of Henry Wood, the village saddler. At least his time working in Sampford Peverell had provided him with the contact necessary to ensure future employment.

The freehold of the Ghost House was sold to William Thomas for £230, with Maria's children receiving their inheritance from the proceeds of sale, although the mortgage-holders and solicitors received the largest share. The 1891 census shows William Conde Thomas, his wife, Elizabeth, son Charles aged 5, father-in-law Samuel Wading, nephew Samuel Wading and Johanna Webber, a boarder aged 73 living at the property.

Initially, business could not have been too good for William Thomas because on 22 December 1892 Charles Upcott and Edward Gillard, businessmen from Cullompton, threatened legal action over the sum of £85 owed for goods supplied which William Thomas was unable to pay. A 'riding mortgage'[1] was drawn up for the sum of £85 plus another £35 with which, no doubt, he thought he could work his way out of trouble. William Thomas appears to have been successful from then on. In 1899, when in need of further finance, he took out a new mortgage for £450 and redeemed both of his existing mortgages totalling £320. A property valuation survey carried out in 1910[2] provides some more detail about the premises: "Cob and thatch shop, house and bakery. Contains ground floor shop, 3 sitting rooms, kitchen, coal [store built of] cob. First floor 4 bedrooms. Outside an old cottage now used as stable and store. Garden. Store of grass with 2 stone and tile fowl-houses. Very old and in poor repair".

William Thomas died in 1911 aged 53 leaving his son Charles, then aged 25, as heir to what appears to have been a very successful business. Shortly before he died, the census shows William and Charles as bakers, Albert Knight and William Milton as baker's assistants, plus Elizabeth Thomas, Charles' wife, and Minnie May his daughter as shop/bakery assistants. After William's death, Charles and Minnie took over the business, and ran it between them for over 40 years.

Denis Cluett who, later in his life, wrote about his memories of the village between 1909 and 1919, recalled the small baker's shop known as Thomas's:

> Although I suppose most people baked their own bread, the shop was always handy if one wanted yeast cakes or an extra loaf or two. They sold two kinds of loaf - tinned and cottage. I remember we used to buy tinned loaves if we were going for a picnic or having a party since bread for sandwiches could be cut much more easily and tidily from the baker's tinned loaf. They also used to make miniature cottage loaves known as milk loaves, so called because the dough was mixed with milk instead of water. They used to sell these for one farthing and we bought and ate them hot from the oven. They were delicious. The village also relied upon Thomas the baker for their hot cross buns, delivered before breakfast still hot from the oven, on the morning of Good Friday.

A newspaper article of 1929 reports that at 10 o'clock on a Wednesday morning Mr Thomas went out into the yard and spotted the thatched roof on fire. The ground floor furniture was removed with the help of neighbours but the bedroom furniture was all lost. Charlie and Minnie moved across the road to the middle of three cottages which were attached to "Marble Arch"(the name ascribed by postcard photographers to a particular cottage with an upstairs room that spanned the lane to Sampford Barton), and another bakery was built on the site of the old one. The new bakery was single storey with a pitched roof, with the oven built outside the bakehouse. The coal-fired oven was lit every day, including Sundays, right up until the 1950s. Coal was stored in the yard in a heap and bucketfuls carried down as needed.

It seemed that the brother and sister were to be dogged by bad luck because in March 1939 the cottage in which they were living, opposite the bakery, caught fire and was burned to the ground, along with the other cottages on that site. Consequently, Charlie and his sister moved again, this time to part of London House, Higher Town, where they were living when the 1939 Register was compiled[6]. Charlie was described as a master bread maker and poultry farmer, with Minnie as baker's assistant. Their stay at London House may have been a short-term arrangement to help them through their emergency, as they subsequently lived in one of the cottages in Back Lane, No 17 Higher Town. In 1933 16-year-old Len Maynard began work at the bakery and remained there most of his working life, except for a brief spell during WW2. One of Len's younger brothers, Victor (known as Vic) Maynard, joined him in 1941 when he started full-time work. Prior to this Vic had worked part-time helping look after the chickens on land that ran from behind the bakery right down to Turnpike.

GHOST HOUSE GUTTED

Destructive Fire at Sampford Peverell

Ghost House, Sampford Peverell, a dwelling and shop, tenanted by Mr. Charles Thomas, and said to be nearly 400 years old, was destroyed by fire on Wednesday. The outbreak was noticed by Mr. Thomas when he went into the yard at about 10 o'clock.

Tiverton Fire Brigade was summoned, and arriving promptly, brought four powerful jets to bear on the house. The fire, however, had obtained a firm hold, and the falling in of the roof was soon followed by the collapse of the end wall. The thatch of a cottage across the narrow roadway was ignited, but this additional outbreak was quickly dealt with.

Ghost House was a cob and thatch dwelling comprising eight rooms and a shop. Living with Mr. Thomas was his sister, Miss M. Thomas. The place is reputed to have been the scene of all kinds of weird happenings in bygone days, and on some of the windows inscriptions had been scratched by a former tenant named Bellamy, whose name is perpetuated in the parish church.

Western Times, 13 September 1929. Image reproduced with kind permission of The British Newspaper Archive (www.britishnewspaperarchive.co.uk) Image ©THE BRITISH LIBRARY BOARD, ALL RIGHTS RESERVED.

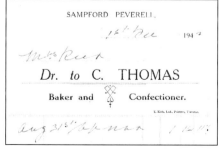

Thomas' billhead, 1940s
Courtesy of Martin Reid

Fire Destroys three cottages. Express & Echo, 28 March 1939.

Vic Maynard recollected that the Thomases were of short stature, being about 5'2" tall. Minnie was a staunch Methodist and saw no evil in anyone, often giving bread away to those she thought in need. Charlie was the more business-minded of the two. Also a Methodist, Charlie loved to play Napoleon, a card game that first appeared in the 19th century. So fond of 'Nap' was he that as a youngster he and his friends would play cards in the balcony of the Methodist Chapel during services.

The baker's working day began at 4.00am. Flour, delivered in 1.5cwt or 2cwt sacks from Hamley's Mill in St Andrew Street, Tiverton, was brought in from the wooden storage shed at the rear of the bakehouse and fresh yeast, delivered in 3lb lumps contained in cotton bags from Renshaw's (a nationwide company which also supplied fat and fruit for cakes), was mixed in a steel drum that was turned by hand. Water was carried up by yoke and buckets from the pump in Boobery.

The dough was then turned out into a large wooden trough where it would be proved and 'knocked back' twice. Then it was hand cut and weighed into 1lb, 2lb or 4lb (quartern) tins (greased with liquid lard painted on with

The single storey bakery, 1950s

a brush) which were arrayed on the floor of the bakery. 120 tins of dough were left to prove once again. Using a 'peel', a flat wooden shovel with a 10-foot handle, Charlie would load his coal-fired oven which had been brought up to temperature and the fire let go out, and bake his bread. The process took 6 hours from beginning to end. When the peel became a little blunt and wouldn't slide easily under the tins Charlie's language turned the air blue. His sister would remind him if children were near. Charlie merely swore at the children.

There was no actual shop on the bakery premises but customers would just call at the door for bread, fruit cake or Madeira cake, or relied upon the delivery van, which was driven by Charlie, Minnie or Len. They delivered as far as Stag Mill and Beerdown beyond Uplowman, often not returning home until 8.00 or 9.00pm, making the working day 18 hours long.

Customers generally paid weekly although Minnie was inclined to be very lenient and probably gave away more than she sold. Prices were kept artificially low, 2½d for a 2lb loaf to ensure the poor always had something to eat. Also, as the oven had to be lit 7 days a week, on Sundays villagers were allowed to bring their roast dinners to be cooked in the bakery oven.

This practice continued well into the 1950s when the oven became oil-fired and most domestic houses had their own ovens.

During the war Charlie baked quartern loaves for the big US Army camp in Tiverton, which boosted his income, and he also made doughnuts for the American troops based locally who preferred his to those available in their camp.

Some of the boys who attended the St Boniface Home in the village had fond memories of Thomas's bakery. Mike Bussell and John Blake, who were there in the late 1940s, recalled that "the smell of bread from the baker's next to the school was irresistible for the hungry boys. They would keep back some coins which they were supposed to leave in the Church collection, in order to buy a hot, white loaf for one penny and three farthings." When Charlie eventually retired, Len Maynard, then living at Wharf House which belonged to Henry Wood, the saddler, took over the business. Charlie Thomas died in 1956. Len ran the bakery - his speciality being pasties - and for many years, employed two of his sisters and latterly also George Grant.

George Grant was born in Payhembury in 1911. Both he and his brother were bakers and George moved to London where he became a Master Baker. He came back to join his brother who ran two baker's shops in Cullompton but eventually felt it was time to go it alone. In 1955 he, his wife and young son, Kevin, moved to Sampford Peverell and lodged with Len Maynard at Wharf House for a year, then moved to Mill Cottage for another two or three years and finally ended up at 17 Higher Town.

In the late 1950s Len decided to give up the bakery business and, together with his brothers Peter and Vic, became an electrician. Meanwhile George

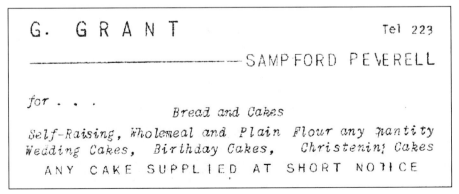

G. GRANT   Tel 223

—————————————————————— SAMPFORD PEVERELL

for . . .
                    Bread and Cakes
Self-Raising, Wholemeal and Plain Flour any quantity
Wedding Cakes, Birthday Cakes, Christening Cakes
   ANY CAKE SUPPLIED AT SHORT NOTICE

Parish magazine advertisement, December 1957

Grant took over Sampford Peverell Bakery, still operating from the Ghost House premises.

George and his wife worked an 18-hour day, George rising at 3.00am to set the dough machine going and his wife joining him in the bakehouse at about 5.00am when the cakes were made. His advertisements in the Parish Magazine showed that besides bread, cakes, wholemeal and plain flour in any quantity, and celebration cakes, "any cake" could be "supplied at short notice."

Their son Kevin helped out at weekends and school holidays. One day whilst making a delivery to a house in Boobery, George broke his ankle and was forced to give up the business. Kevin had no interest in baking, having just begun his apprenticeship as an electrician, thereby ending the Grants' involvement in the bakery business. Tiverton Council subsequently ruled that the Ghost House was no longer fit for use as a bakery and all the equipment, property and land was sold off by Minnie Thomas in 1962. The land, originally a burgage plot that ran from Higher Town down to Turnpike, was bought by Joyce Selley, Vic Maynard's sister (and later a very popular school dinner lady), and her husband Albert, and the old bakehouse was abandoned for several years. In 1973, Vic, who had progressed from being an electrician to becoming an engineer for Indesit, branched out with his wife Anita to form their own business, V & A Maynard.

Vic used the empty bakehouse as storage for washing machines and refrigerators. That storage facility is still within the original walls of the bakehouse, which was modified to remove its windows and replace the pitched roof with a pent one. In 1988 Peter Adcock joined the business and subsequently married the boss's daughter, Karen. The building still had the old baking ovens in place and Peter helped to remove them.

Joyce and Albert Selley sold off a large portion of their land and were then able to have a bungalow built on the site, set back from the road, behind the storage facility. They employed Wright & Sharland, a local building firm. After both Albert and Joyce died, Peter and Karen Adcock bought the bungalow and had an upper floor added. The original property had been so well built than no extra ground work was needed to support the additional weight.

Vic finally retired from business in 2000 passing it to his son-in-law and daughter who continue to this day, still trading as V & A Maynard, and still using the storage facility as a warehouse for white goods.

Other Bakers

4 Higher Town - Southwood's Bakery

Richard and Thomas were two of the sons of Richard and Fanny Southwood, and were born in Sampford Peverell in 1801 and 1805 respectively. Although nothing is known of their early lives, by 1836, upon the baptism of his first child, Richard was described as a baker. He lived with his wife Elizabeth at Key Head (now Quay Head) in Boobery. His brother Thomas lived at one end of a complex of four cottages known as Skinners, situated in Higher Town opposite the turning to Boobery (now part of the garden of 4 Higher Town). The cottage that Thomas rented was by far the largest of the four, having the bakehouse, other outhouses and the garden.

From later records, notably the Tithe Apportionments of 1844 and a newspaper advertisement of 1868, it is clear that a bakery had operated from Skinners from the mid 1830s. It is likely that the brothers ran the business from there, and that Key Head was used solely as a private residence for Richard Southwood and his family.

Although Thomas Southwood remained unmarried, he did have apprentices, or other unmarried bakers, live and work with him. Those that we know of are shown in the censuses: in 1841 there was 15-year-old Joseph Sparkes; in 1851 there were 24-year-old James Holway, a cousin, and 18-year-old John Collins, a nephew. By 1851, Richard's family comprised his wife Elizabeth, his sons William Stone Wood (aged 15) and Richard (aged 6), together with his daughters Laura (aged 13) and Jane (aged 9). The census of that year shows that the eldest child, William, had moved to Lands Mill in Uplowman to work for his widowed grandmother, Jane Wood, as a miller.

The bakery business continued to do well, with the brothers working in partnership, until 1860, when Thomas died. A successor for the business had to be found, and it would seem that Richard's eldest son William was settled in his career as a miller. Richard's other children were probably either too young (his son Richard was just 15), or inexperienced. The person chosen was the brothers' nephew, George Collins (mentioned in the section on the Ghost House bakery). The son of an agricultural labourer, he had been brought up in Boobery, Sampford Peverell, but had learned the

Richard Southwood's signature on 1852 petition   *Courtesy of findmypast.co.uk*

trade of a baker. In the 1851 census he was working for Herman Symons, a baker and confectioner in Bampton Street, Tiverton. Perhaps he had already been working as an employee of the Southwood family during the 1850s, but it was not until 1861 that there are records to show that he became the baker at Skinners, which he leased from the trustees of Thomas Southwood's estate.

When 30-year-old George Collins took over the bakery, he moved in to Skinners with his wife Maria, aged 23, and one employee, William Hill. Around the same time Richard Southwood, now 60, gave up being a baker and became a gardener.

The situation remained the same until September 1868, when George Collins bought the Ghost House, also in Higher Town, and set up a new bakery there. Perhaps this was precipitated by the desire for Richard Southwood junior to take over the bakery business at Skinners now that he was 23 years old. Whatever the cause, George Collins moved out and Richard Southwood junior moved in. Then in November of the same year, a few days after Richard Southwood snr had died, the 4 cottages that comprised Skinners were put up for auction, together with three other lots of property assets. The description for Lot 1 is as follows:

> All those 4 dwelling houses with bake house, outhouses, and excellent walled gardens, in respective occupations of Messrs Southwood, Ryder, Parker and Lovell. This lot is freehold and is situated in Fore Street Sampford Peverell aforesaid, and is let at £20 per annum or thereabouts. The baking business has been successfully carried on in the premises for more than 30 years.

The outcome of the auction is not recorded, but Richard Southwood junior did become the new owner and baker at Skinners in partnership with his sister Jane. What is unclear is whether George Collins at the Ghost House and Richard Southwood at Skinners, who were cousins, were in competition with each other or were working co-operatively at this time. In April 1870 both George Collins and Richard Southwood were summoned by Superintendent Collins for selling bread which was too light in weight. The cases were brought because the Holcombe bakers had complained to Supt Collins that the Sampford bakers were selling their bread too cheaply. George Collins was accused of selling a loaf other than by weight, which proved to be half an ounce too light. He said he was not aware that he had to weigh the bread unless requested. Supt Collins said George Collins was of very good character and nobody had complained about him before, so he was only fined one shilling and costs.

In the other case on the same day, as reported in the Western Times on 14 April 1870, Richard Southwood's older sister Jane, his partner in the bakery, gave a spirited defence, but they did not escape so lightly:

> PC Ryder said he sent a little girl to Mr Southwood's shop to purchase a small loaf, on the 7th inst., about 9 pm, and waited close by until she came with it. He gave her a penny for fetching it, weighed it and found it 1oz 10 dr[ams] too light. Eliza Jane Hodder, a girl of about 10 years of age, said she went and purchased the loaf and gave it to Mr Ryder, he gave her a penny for fetching it ... She paid 2½d for it. Miss Southwood in the absence of her brother, answered to the charge and said the bread was full weight when she delivered it to the girl, that the loaf was stale when weighed, that this case would not have been brought against her brother and herself (partners) but for spite, and she did not think it right for a policeman to give a child a penny to fetch a loaf of bread and tell a falsehood when she came for it, for on being asked who it was for she said she did not know ... The Bench said it was a serious charge and that a former conviction appeared against defendants for a like offence. Fined £1 12s 6d including costs.

Two years after acquiring the premises and commencing his business there, now aged 26, Richard married recently-widowed Caroline Taylor, who was keeping a shop across the road at Chorleys. Richard's life had changed dramatically in just a few years. The story of Richard and Caroline is continued in the chapter on Grocers and Drapers.

In 1871 Richard and his sister Jane were both working as bakers in Higher Town, probably in Skinners, but Jane died in 1876. Skinners was then left vacant and its condition deteriorated to the extent that it was reported to be in ruins in 1904 and was demolished soon afterwards.

14 Higher Town - Grocer's shop

Details about this long-established grocer's shop are to be found in a separate chapter. However, it should be noted here that the shop was owned and run by bakers from about 1894 to 1930, firstly under Samuel Holloway, then by William Chidgey. They both included bakery goods among their range of products, and, according to the 1910 survey[2], there was a bakehouse at the premises. In William Chidgey's case, he had another bakery in Halberton, so may have split the production between the two premises.

6 Chains Road – Bennett's Bakery

John Bennett is first mentioned in the records for Sampford Peverell in 1847, when he was listed on the Electoral Roll as the tenant occupier of 'Saunders'. This was a large property in Chains Road, at that time divided into two households, which was redeveloped in 1900 to become Norrish's Creamery. In the 1851 census he was shown to be 41 years old, a baker employing one person, born in Culmstock and married. His wife Mary, 28, was born in Hemyock. Living with them were Eliza Lock, a servant aged 18, and Henry Quant, 17, an errand boy.

During the 1850s, he must have made the acquaintance of John Richard Chave, who ran a school a few doors away from him at Sheppards House (now the Merriemeade public house). The story of Mr Chave's school, and its demise when he became bankrupt, is detailed in 'The Schools of Sampford Peverell: Two Centuries of Education'. In 1859, when Mr Chave's debts began to overwhelm him, he arranged to assign all his real and personal estate to John Bennett, and one other, as trustees, so that they could reach some agreement with his creditors. One can imagine that this was far from a straightforward matter, because it was still being resolved through the courts five years later, as reported in the Exeter Flying Post on 20 April 1864.

Chains Road, 1890s. Saunders is the white thatched house on the right

John Bennett's signature on 1852 petition
Courtesy of findmypast.co.uk

By the 1861 census, the Bennetts had had two children: John, aged 2, and William aged 8 months who died shortly afterwards. They had an 18-year-old journeyman baker living with them at the time - Benjamin Calbraith from Sampford Peverell. One of John Bennett's interests, it would seem, was education. He was one of the initial subscribers for shares in the Sampford Peverell Middle School (later re-named East Devon County School), and his name appears as an attendee at several of the early meetings. Perhaps he hoped to enrol his son, John, at the School when he was older.

Another court case involving John Bennett was reported in the Tiverton Gazette on 20 December 1864. On this occasion he was the plaintiff, and he was suing Robert Jacobs, a Sampford Peverell butcher, for £8 18s. 1d. This was for bread supplied over a period of 9 years, which gives some insight as to how business was conducted at that time. The defendant pleaded that his 'circumstances were very low' and that 'if the plaintiff wanted anything of him, he must take his body for he had nothing else to give'. On being pressed, he agreed that he could pay 1s. 6d. per month, but John Bennett thought he could afford more. The case was referred to arbitration.

At Cullompton Petty Sessions, as reported in the Tiverton Gazette on 2 March 1875, John Bennett himself was on trial, accused of providing underweight bread. His son had delivered four 1 pound loaves to Mr Thomas at the Halfway House Inn in Willand. On being weighed, they were found to be 3 ounces short of weight. Mr Bennett's response was that the loaves were 'fancy bread' made expressly for Mr Thomas. "He would not divide a quartern loaf into 4 loaves and guarantee that each should be 1 lb, not even for Her Majesty the Queen" (to which there was reported to be laughter). He was fined a token amount of 6d. and had to pay costs of 10s.

After John died in 1878, his widow, Mary, took over as the baker at Saunders. From the 1881 census, it can be seen that she had assistance from another baker, 19-year-old John Parker, of Sampford Peverell. She carried on in business until about 1890, this being the last year in which local directories list her as a baker. It would seem that she then retired and Saunders was divided into two parts, each being known as 'Saunders Cottage'. Mary lived in one part, whilst Edward Cottey, a 22 year old baker and confectioner, had taken over the bakery and lived in the other part. However, it is not listed in the local directories as a commercial premises, so perhaps he was working for someone else. By 1901[7], he had moved away and the property had been redeveloped as Norrish's Creamery.

Lower Town - Coles' Bakery

John Coles (Lower Town) is listed in the 1841 census as a baker. John lived in one of five cottages which stood near the entrance to where Court Way is now situated. There is no evidence that he worked from his home nor that he had premises elsewhere, but by the 1851 census John Coles was listed as baker and inn keeper at the New Inn in Higher Town, now two private dwellings. He had given up his baking business by 1857, when he was described as a Victualler and Farmer.

Higher Town and Mount Pleasant - Taylor's Bakery

George Taylor was the son of John Taylor, a farmer turned shopkeeper, and his second wife Caroline. They ran the shop in Chorleys, now named Paulett House (9 Higher Town). George's father died in 1869 and his mother married Richard Southwood, a baker mentioned earlier. They initially lived in Richard Southwood's house (since demolished) at 4 Higher Town, but later moved to 9 Higher Town which Caroline had inherited from Richard Southwood. George Taylor continued the family business becoming a baker in the same premises; he was living there in 1891 with his wife Lucy and two 17-year-old bakers, Frederick Parr and Tom Knowles.

Two years later, Kelly's Directory of 1893 shows that George had moved to Mount Pleasant, Whitnage Road. He continued as a baker (later described as farmer and baker) until 1909 when a fire destroyed part of his property, as reported in Western Times on 6 Aug 1909. Whilst Mr Taylor was out, a fire took hold in the bakehouse, which was part of the farmhouse, the fire only having been discovered upon his return. Although he was insured, this put an end to his baking business, and thereafter his occupation was as a farmer only.

There are other men who on various censuses describe themselves as bakers, but as they only appear briefly in the records of the village we have to assume that they were employees rather than bakers in their own right.

Chapter 3

Butchers

Introduction

The butchers' trade goes back to when people first started keeping livestock, when specialists in rearing, slaughtering and dealing with meat became needed. Organisations of butchers existed in Anglo-Saxon times: a "Butchers' Hall where the craftsmen meet" is recorded in London in 975 AD. A butchers' guild is recorded in York in 1272, and it includes the names of 'freemen butchers', i.e. men who had served an apprenticeship as a butcher and had qualified to trade in their own right. In Exeter there was a system of overseeing the sale of meat in markets: in 1384 butchers elected wardens to supervise the town's meat market, known as the Fleshfold. Butchers' guilds were responsible for such matters as hygiene, weights and measures, checking sales of meat on restricted or fast days, and looking out for non-guild butchers. They also protected standards of workmanship through the apprenticeship system.

Traders in towns tended to congregate in areas according to their trade, and the butchers' area was often called the Shambles, a shamble being

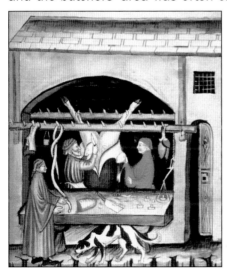

Medieval butcher's shop

an old word for the stall or bench on which meat was displayed. A mid-17th century survey of properties in Sampford Peverell includes a 'Burgage called the Little Shambles' occupied by James Pringe. In the 1696 survey 'Little Shambles', a three acre burgage plot, is occupied by Robert Wine, and in both the 1700 survey and an undated 18th century survey we have Joane Hall and Phillip and Joane Evans in 'one Cottage and ½ acre of land Little Shambles'. In an 18th century survey there is also a 'messuage or Burgage Close called Little Shambles' occupied by

Elizabeth and Nick King, John Farr, and Elizabeth Bidgood with a comment about the property lying within the ring fence of Sampford Farm and that the lease ought to be granted with the farm in future, so perhaps it was an outlet for meat from Sampford Barton.

We have the names of some early Sampford Peverell butchers from bastardy orders (orders to pay support for children they had fathered out of wedlock), from marriage licences issued in Exeter, and from apprenticeship records. The earliest of these dates from 1670, when Robert Drewe, butcher, was ordered by the Overseers of the Poor for Sampford Peverell to pay 10d a week to support Mary, the illegitimate daughter of Grace Manley.

The next was in 1725 when Hugh Langham of Sampford Peverell, butcher, married Joan Marsh by licence. This was probably the same Hugh Langham, son of John Langham, who was baptised in Sampford Peverell in October 1684 and who died in 1768. In 1763 a John Langham, butcher, took on Daniel Jutsum as an apprentice, so it seems likely that this John Langham was related to Hugh Langham as families often followed the same trade. Another butcher from Sampford Peverell to marry by licence was Nicholas Rowe, who married Betty Poole in 1736 and had a son, also Nicholas, who was baptised in the parish church in April of the following year. He may have been related to Thomas Rowe, a trustee and executor of the 1754 will of Henry Dawbney, in which he is described as a butcher.

One more local butcher from this period, William Chave, married Mary Norrish by licence in 1741. In 1744 their son, William, was baptised in the church. A year later, a bastardy order required William Chave, butcher, to pay an initial sum of 27 shillings, and then 10d a week to support the illegitimate baby daughter of Margaret Kerslake. According to the 1744/45 Land Tax records he owned a property called Smyths. William Chave died in 1748.

Apart from their names and the few scant details that are shown above, nothing more is known about these early butchers of Sampford Peverell. Indeed, it is not until the beginning of the 19th century that sufficient records exist for us to be able to provide a narrative about them, which follows in the remainder of this chapter.

12 Lower Town – Challis

The property in Lower Town known for most of its recorded history simply as "Challis" is not to be confused with "Challis House" (next door), or "Challis Cottage" (next door to that), which feature elsewhere in this volume - in the story of 8 and 10 Lower Town. The building we're concerned with here (together with outbuildings to the rear) is set behind iron railings, has bay windows on either side of the entrance, and adjoins the access road leading to the rear of the Globe Inn. At the time our 'story' starts, it is likely that a cottage or farmhouse occupied the site, since the present 3-storey house is believed to date from the 1880s.

The first reference we have to its commercial life is in the Land Tax Returns of 1825, when the property was known as "Shallis", owned and occupied by William Pine. He is known to have been a butcher by trade because a notice addressed "To the Debtors and Creditors of William Pine late of Sampford Peverell, in the County of Devon, Butcher, deceased" appeared in the Western Times of 22 October 1831.

The Land Tax Return for 1832 shows that the new owner was William Wood, and the occupier was Richard Shackell, although an absence of records from around this period means that one can't be certain that he took over as a butcher straight away. However, when the Census was conducted in 1841 it is clear that the premises were, by then, occupied by Richard Shackell (butcher) with his wife Ann (née Beedell) and their young family – including the eldest son Richard, then 4 years old, a journeyman butcher named John Perram, and two servants.

Richard (senior) was a farmer as well as a butcher, and was not without a sense of humour; the following story was published in provincial newspapers nationwide in February 1842:

EXTRAORDINARY INVITATION.—" Mr. Richard Shackell very kindly invites those persons who have already taken a part of his turnips from a field known by the name of Townsend-field, to attend on the said premises between the hours of ten and twelve o'clock this day, when he will be there for the purpose of delivering the remaining part. Only the persons who have taken the others will be expected." The above was published by the crier through the village of Sampford Peverell on the 21st of January.—*Western Times.*

Kentish Gazette, 22 February 1842.

Richard and Ann had another child, James, in 1843, but Ann died that same year, possibly in childbirth, and Richard senior died in 1850. The older boys (then 13 and 11) being clearly too young to take over the business, Richard's mother Sarah stepped in to run the shop and look after the boys.

Sarah's nephew, William Shackell, also a butcher, lived and worked with them[3]. Sarah herself died in 1851, which seems to have brought an end to the Shackell family's tenure of this

William Shackell's signature on 1852 petition
Courtesy of findmypast.co.uk

business. However, young Richard must have entered into the family trade, because in 1871 we find him as a "Master Butcher" at 37 Brompton Road, Kensington, with his wife Kate and young family.

By 1856 the butchery business at Challis had passed to John Bowden, the son of Thomas Bowden, farmer, of Lower Town, Sampford Peverell, and his wife Harriett[4]. He was a "Butcher's Apprentice" in the household of John Fisher, another Lower Town farmer, in 1851, and married Grace Ponsford (daughter of Richard Ponsford – yet another Lower Town farmer) in 1857. John and Grace Bowden did not have any children, but they had a succession of live-in apprentices assisting in the business: John Morgan in 1861, Walter Bray in 1871 (he later became John Bowden's brother-in-law), and Robert Fowler in 1881.

The Bowdens had been renting the property from the trustees of Richard Gunn, deceased, and in 1884 the trustees gave directions for Mr Gunn's properties, including Challis, to be sold at auction. As a result of the sale, and having no sons in the butchery business, John and Grace Bowden moved into Globe Cottage, which was later renamed 'Providence House' and subsequently incorporated into the Globe Inn.

The successful bidder for Challis was William J Williams, who paid £210 for the property, which was described thus: "The dwelling-house, with shop, yard, slaughter-house, barn, stabling, cow-sheds, piggery, and large garden, situate in the village [of Sampford Peverell] and extending from the high road to the Canal, occupied by Mr John Bowden".

AUCTION THIS DAY.

SAMPFORD PEVERELL, NEAR TIVERTON,

2¼ Miles from Tiverton Junction and Burlescombe Stations of the Great Western Railway.

MESSRS. BEST and COMMIN are instructed by the Trustees under the Will of Richard Gunn, deceased, to SELL by AUCTION, at the Palmerston Hotel, Tiverton, This Day (Tuesday), 14th of October, 1884, at Half-past Three o'clock in the Afternoon precisely, the following FREEHOLD OVERLAND TENEMENT and MESSUAGES :—

Lot 1.—Three arable fields, three pasture fields, and orchard, adjoining each other containing 15a. 0r. 23p., situate on the south-eastern side of the Great-Western Canal, now and for many years in the occupation of Mr. John Bowden, as yearly tenant from Lady-day.

Lot 2.—A pasture field, known as Netherton Meadow, containing 4a. 3r., near to Lot 1, also occupied by Mr. John Bowden.

Lot 3.—The dwelling-house, with shop, yard, slaughter-house, barn, stabling, cow-sheds, piggery, and large garden, situate in the village, and extending from the high road to the Canal, also occupied by Mr. John Bowden.

Lot 4.—The modern dwelling-house, shop and stores, yard, and large garden, adjoining Lot 3, in the occupation of Mr. Tandevin, grocer and draper.

The Properties may be viewed on application to the respective Tenants, and particulars, with plan and conditions of Sale, may be obtained of the AUCTIONEERS, Qu—a-street-road, Exeter; or of Mr. G. W. Cockram, Solicitor, Tiverton.

Exeter & Plymouth Gazette 14 October 1884.

William J Williams already had a butcher's business in the village before he bought Challis. A brief obituary, which appeared in the Exeter & Plymouth Gazette following his death in 1938 includes the following information:

> Born in Uffculme [in 1850] Mr Williams was apprenticed to a butcher, the late Mr Philip Trott, and later went to London. Not long afterwards he went to America, and found employment in a meat-packing works in Chicago. He was only there two years, but in that time he bought a piece of land, which he sold at a profit, and returned to England.

It reports that he opened his business as a butcher in Sampford Peverell in 1874. His grand-daughter, Stella Newcombe, in an interview in 2004, told us that he returned from America after "making his fortune", and built the three-storey house called "Challis" which stands today.

In 1875 he married Eliza Wright, daughter of a Hemyock dairyman, and they had six children during the course of the next 16 years. Between 1878 and 1883 he was both a butcher in, and the licensee of, the 'Hare and Hounds' in Lower Town[5]. Living there with him were Eliza, their first son (also William J Williams) and a 19-year-old "Butcher's Apprentice", Robert Quick. Combining the two trades of butcher and licensee was not exceptional, although in William Williams' case, it was not to last.

Challis circa 1908

It was probably very soon after William Williams bought 'Challis' in 1884 that he had the old dwelling-house there demolished, and built a new three-storey house in its place. In 1886, the licence for the 'Hare & Hounds' was transferred to Frederick Dunn, so it was probably then that the Williams family moved into their splendid new house. By the time of the census in 1891, the family, now with six children, including 1-month-old Stanley (who would later take over the business), an "Apprentice Butcher", Thomas Northam, a "Servant Butcher", Robert Wood and two domestic servants, have what is clearly a thriving business at "Challis".

The 1910 Survey gives a full description of the premises at that time, as follows:

> Stone, stucco and slated house and shop (Butchers) with buildings and (5 acre) meadow near. House contains: ground floor shop, private entrance, sitting room, kitchen, office; first floor 3 bedrooms and bathroom; second floor 3 bedrooms. Yard in rear with larder, washhouse and store over; stone, brick and slate slaughterhouse, salting house, harness room. Galvanised iron linhay, stone and slate range, bullock house (2), stable (3) and mealhouse. Stone and slate piggery, stone and tile cow pens (10) and chaff house. Stone ground floor piggery and earth closet in garden behind. House good, buildings fair repair. Water meadow near of good quality.

Stella recalled that William had four sons who worked in the butchery with him "for minimal wages", and that when they married, he set each of them up in a farm for a living. She said that "This was the usual way of doing things in those days", and although Stella's father Stanley was the youngest son, he gave him Challis - with the butchery. The eldest son William John, was a "butcher and farmer" in Uffculme by 1911. The other three sons were still living at home then. Herbert (aged 29) was described as "Working in the Business". He married Grace Goffin in 1914 and by

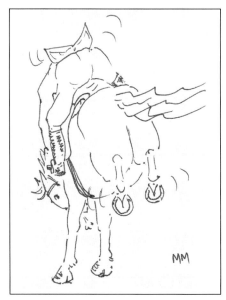

Riding a Canadian horse - unsuccessfully!   *Illustration by Maggie Muggleton*

1939 they were living at "Mountain Oak", Sampford Peverell, where his occupation was given as "Farmer (mixed)"[6]. Archibald was described as a "Cattle Dealer". He married Catherine Kemp later in 1911. When Stanley took over his father's business, William J Williams senior retired with his wife to Gore House, Uffculme, where he died in 1938 at the age of 88 – Eliza having died 5 years previously.

Stanley Williams did not, however, take over the butchery business at Challis until after returning from Army service with the Royal Field Artillery in World War I. In 1914 he married Dora Elston from Silverton and the eldest of their three children, Stella, was born in the following year. As a married man, Stanley was not required to enlist at that time, so he must have volunteered to do so when he joined up in December 1915. He became a 'driver' and was in France for 18 months between 1917 and 1919. He was a small man: only 5'4" tall and weighing 130lbs when he was examined on enlistment. Stella recalled that, returning home from the War, her father started breeding Canadian horses alongside the butchery, and that one of her earliest childhood memories is of him trying to ride one up Lower Town – without much success. He later turned to cattle dealing, which became his main occupation in conjunction with the butchery.

Stella also remembered that her father would go to Exeter market, travelling by horse and trap to Tiverton and thence by train to Exeter. Cattle bought by him would then be brought by drovers on foot to Sampford Peverell. Later on, when he owned a car, he was able to go to several markets rather than just the one. The cattle would graze in meadows where Fairfield is now situated, and when ready they would either be slaughtered at Challis for the shop or sold elsewhere.

When Stella was 18 she left Sampford Peverell to train as a nurse. At the hospital in Ottery St Mary, she met Harry Roy Newcombe, known as Roy, who was the sales representative for the family business manufacturing scales.

Stanley Williams' butchers bicycle   *Photo: Peter Bowers*

They married in 1939 just a few days after the outbreak of WWII and began their married life in Exeter, living with Roy's parents at 8 Bartholomew Street. While Roy was on military service Stella returned to Sampford Peverell, where her father had bought her a house in Higher Town, "Challis" by then being occupied by Arthur Marley ("Butcher (Manager)") and his wife Hilda, while Stanley, described as "Farmer, Butcher and Cattle Dealer" and Dora, were at "Moor End House".

Roy was in the Army in Gibraltar, but developed stomach ulcers and came home. Stanley retired, leaving Stella and Roy to run the business – such as it was, with meat then being rationed. It is not known precisely when the Newcombes replaced the Marleys at Challis. Stella recalled that for many years her father Stan still went up to the shop every day - possibly because (as she told us) she hated the business (and perhaps Roy did as well).

After the war, social and retail change had adverse effects on the shop and in 1961 they closed it down and moved to Moorend, possibly to live with her parents. Stella then went back to nursing in Tiverton. Stanley died in 1968, aged 77, and Dora in 1975, aged 84.

However, this was not quite the end of the retail meat industry for the village: Roy and Stella had had a very able assistant, Arthur Wheeler (whom they called "Arty"), working for them for five years in the 1950s until he moved to Crediton to run his own butcher's shop there, and in 1964 he returned to Sampford Peverell, purchased the business from Roy Newcombe and reopened the shop at Challis. The house and outbuildings remained the property of the Newcombes, who also kept a few sheep behind the house – as well as a slaughter-house and "sausage-house".

Williams & Newcombe billhead 1959   *Courtesy of Martin Reid*

Arthur's wife Doreen (née Bright – they married in 1951) recalled that when the family returned to the village they at first rented Little Garth Cottage, in Boobery, from Mrs Hirschfeld, who lived in the main house, to which the cottage was attached, but with only 2 bedrooms it was too small for a family of two adults and three children and they moved, first to a council house further up the road, and later to 32 Higher Town.

The shop had no outside signage - not even the name "Wheeler's" over the door. Arthur never advertised the business in the local press, although adverts appeared regularly in the Parish News between 1967 and 1971, and the delivery van was similarly unmarked. Doreen suggested that perhaps her husband found that he had all the business he could handle (he employed no full-time staff, other than Saturday boys, and was not interested in expansion) with deliveries to Westleigh, Halberton, Uplowman, Holcombe Rogus and outlying areas of Tiverton, in addition to many loyal customers in Sampford.

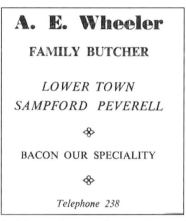

A. E. Wheeler

FAMILY BUTCHER

LOWER TOWN
SAMPFORD PEVERELL

⚗

BACON OUR SPECIALITY

⚗

Telephone 238

Parish magazine advertisement, January 1969

As for the day-to-day running of the business, Doreen recalled that cleanliness and hygiene were of paramount importance to Arthur (although visits from Environmental Health Inspectors were very rare): the shop-floor was washed every day, the old sawdust being swept up first and fresh being laid afterwards, and the hardwood block was scrubbed twice a day, as was the marble slab in the window display.

Doreen drove the delivery van (with occasional help from Rene Middleton and Maureen Guppy); she remembered that it was fitted out with wooden slatted shelves, on which the meat orders were placed – each wrapped in greaseproof paper with the customer's name and address on a pin stuck into it. She made the deliveries, collected the money and took the orders for

FAMILY BUTCHERS

A. E. WHEELER

★ ★ ★

SAMPFORD PEVERELL
DEVON
Telephone 238

Paper bag with Wheeler's logo

35

the following week. Some customers didn't pay C.O.D. (Cash On Delivery) but had a monthly account - sometimes not paid promptly; she thought Arthur was "too soft" on these customers, and a lot of money was still owing when he gave up the business. In fact, his kind heart also led to arguments about Sunday lunch – a customer might come into the shop late on a Saturday, when Arthur had sold all that week's prepared joints, and he would let her have the meat that had been set aside for the family. Doreen's daughter Meryl remembered that her father once sold their Christmas goose to Mrs Thomas on Christmas Eve, leaving the family to celebrate the festive season with a few sausages – although it had to be said that Arthur's sausages were acknowledged to be the best and contained only beef or pork, with nothing added. They were so popular that he made thousands at a time (in the small sausage-house in the yard), hanging them on rails in the large walk-in refrigerator.

He cured his own bacon and ham – green, not smoked – and always cleaned the slicing machine between slicing bacon and ham. He also made his own brawn and faggots, which were cooked in the kitchen and sold to children who would wait for them to be ready so they could eat them fresh from the oven.

Arthur Wheeler   *Courtesy of Doreen Wheeler*

Doreen remembered that her husband was always very charming to his lady customers. Mrs Hirschfeld was partial to fillet steak and always asked "Vill it be nice, Mr Veeler?" Another regular customer was Alice Pengelly, the Newcombes' housekeeper, whose favourite cut was belly pork; one day Arthur saw her coming and had the joint ready for her, having cut off the teats as usual but instead of discarding them had lined them up on the counter to amuse Alice – who always referred to them as 'tats'. Mrs Anne Church (the Colonel's wife from Higher Town) would ask Arthur's advice on what she should buy for Sunday lunch; he would remember what she had had the previous weekend and his suggestion was always accepted.

However, in common with small village shopkeepers everywhere, Arthur Wheeler found that he was unable to compete with the prices and wide selection being offered by larger businesses in nearby towns; nor could he afford to maintain a delivery service (which many customers no longer needed anyway), and 1974 saw the end of "Challis" as a butchery. At about the same time, Arthur had a heart attack and died a year later at Christmas 1975. Doreen moved to a flat in Richmond Close, overlooking the canal, and later to Cullompton, where she now lives.

Roy and Stella Newcombe had sold the premises some years earlier to Wally and Sheila Lamb and had moved to a bungalow off Lower Town. The Lambs put the property on the market with auctioneers "Dobbs, Stagg, Knowlman & Co." for Sale by Auction in February 1973, but two weeks prior to the scheduled sale it was purchased by Graeme and Mary Isaac, who were then operating a Bed & Breakfast business in Witheridge. Arthur Wheeler was a sitting tenant and still trading as a butcher, and he and his family were living in Higher Town. The details in the auctioneer's particulars of that part of the property occupied by the business include the Butchers Shop (18'9" x 11'6" with bay window) and a number of outbuildings, including numerous store rooms, part of an "Old Bacon House" and a "Sausage Room".

The Isaacs spent a year carrying out considerable alterations to the house before moving in early in 1974. Later the same year, Arthur Wheeler ceased trading and Graeme and Mary were able to complete the refurbishment of the property. This included removing the wooden floor of the Butchers Shop – to reveal neat parallel ridges of sawdust where years of daily sweeping had filtered it between the floorboards!

Quay Head, Boobery and 9 Higher Town – Paulett House

James Salter was born in Uffculme in 1867, the son of Joseph Salter, a dairyman, and his wife Emma (née Rowe) also of Uffculme. We don't know where he learnt his trade as a butcher - in 1881 he was 14 and living at home, then Battens Cottage, Halberton – but the Census does not mention an occupation. The cottage was part of Shutehanger Farm, so he was probably familiar with the livestock processes there.

His first appearance in Sampford Peverell's records is in the 1889 Electoral Roll, when he was living at 'Key Head' in Boobery. Kelly's Directory of 1889 and 1890 both establish his trade as a butcher, but without confirmation of his address, which is provided in the Census of 1891. The Census also shows that he was married to Mary Annie, née Cornall, with a 2-year-old daughter, Beatrice, and that living with them was a 16-year-old "Butcher's Servant", James Bowerman.

Key Head circa 1905

'Key Head' is situated next to the stream in Boobery, a feature which would have provided a constant source of running water for the removal of waste from the butchery business. The property still retains a room, adjacent to the stream, which may have been used for meat preparation. From the 1910 survey[2], we know that behind the house, in what is now the garden, were several outbuildings such as pig houses, a chicken house and a slaughterhouse, which would have been an essential part of his business.

Perhaps the location of his shop premises was not ideal, not being on the main thoroughfare in Higher Town where the other shops were situated. When an opportunity presented itself in 1907, James moved to a new building in Higher Town, on the site known as 'Chorleys', which was owned by the Feoffees of the Poor Lands charity. Today, the property is privately owned and is known as 'Paulett House', situated at No. 9 Higher Town. A serious fire in 1902 had destroyed a house and shop at 'Chorleys' occupied by baker Richard Southwood, and three years later (according to the date inscribed on a brick used in its construction) a new house was built on another part of the same plot, which was given the name 'Paulett House'.

Higher Town, Sampford Peverell.

In centre Paulett House, circa 1910

The 1910 survey provides the following description of the property:

Modern, stone, plastered and slated shop (butchers) and house. Ground floor: shop, private entrance, sitting room, 2 kitchens, stone and tile washhouse; 2 stall stable and traphouse in rear. First floor: 4 bedrooms; cellars in basement. Small lawn but no garden.

It is likely that, with the loss of access to running water from the stream at Key Head, James subsequently built a slaughterhouse on the east side of Boobery, a little further downstream from Key Head (by this time known by the new spelling of 'Quay Head'). This is recollected by Denis Cluett in his reminiscences of growing up in the village before and during the Great War[35]:

Butcher Salter's slaughterhouse was situated on the bank of a stream some distance from his shop. During the holidays Reg Russell and I often used to spend a morning watching the animals being slaughtered. Humane killing had not been heard of at this time. Sheep and pigs were killed by the knife, calves were poleaxed and bullocks were shot by a special cartridge fired from a twelve-bore shotgun. On the whole it was a pretty gory business and, as far as the pigs were concerned, a pretty noisy one too. However, we children took it all as a matter of course, and I don't think we were brutalised by something which to us seemed very ordinary and necessary. If we were lucky, Salter would give us a pig's bladder which we could inflate and use as a football.

Quay Head with slaughterhouse on right in foreground, across canal

Denis also provided a description of Salter's butcher's shop, which he considered to be a replica of Williams' at 'Challis' in Lower Town:

> Both were scrupulously clean, and the floors liberally sprinkled with clean sawdust. The main feature in each was the chopping block - a massive section of a tree trunk. There were no refrigerators and the whole carcasses of the animals were hung around the shop to be laid on the block and chopped up as required. Joints were always sold complete with the bone. The two butchers always dressed alike in snowy white shirts with the sleeves rolled up above the elbows, a blue and white striped apron girt about the waist with a length of thin rope from which hung a selection of knives and a sharpening steel. They both wore breeches with black leggings and boots, both of which were always polished to a mirror finish. The whole ensemble was topped off with a straw boater.

Although Denis Cluett said that there were no refrigerators, Salter's shop did possess one, albeit without electrification, in the basement. A walk-in cold store, complete with meat hooks fixed to the ceiling, was still to be found at the property in 2018.

Butchers' block   Illustration by Kathleen Homles

James Salter's daughter Beatrice married a teacher in 1914 and moved away, while his son Edmund remained at home assisting his father in the business, except for his period of service during the First World War. He served in the Army Service Corps and the Devonshire Regiment, spending over two years in Egypt, finally being discharged, wounded, in July 1919. Tragically for the family and the business, Edmund died in 1929, at the very young age of 36. Only a few months later, James Salter lost his wife Mary, who died aged 65. James must have been devastated, but continued to trade at Paulett House for a few more years, and the last Directory listing for him is in 1935. He retired to Wharf Cottage, Turnpike, where we find him on the 1939 Register living with his housekeeper Irene Manley. He died in 1940, aged 73.

At some point after 1935, James Salter's butchery business at Paulett House was acquired by Jack Popham – listed on the 1939 Register as "Butcher Shopkeeper (own account)". He was born in Bow, Devon, on the last day of December 1892, the son of John Popham, "police officer" and his wife Emma[7].

In 1911 he was at Aldershot, aged 18, under training for service in the Army Service Corps, his occupation on the Census form given as "Butcher". He served in WW1 as a "Transport Sergeant" in the A.S.C. He married Florence M. Davis in 1921 and in 1939 she was living with him at Paulett; they don't appear to have had any children. Jack Popham's tenure at Paulett House was short lived, because he died in 1941. Since then, the premises have been used as a private house.

Other Butchers

Apart from the principal businesses centred on Quay Head/Paulett House (Salter and Popham) and Challis (Pine, Shackell, Bowden, Williams, Newcombe and Wheeler), previously described, Trade Directories and Censuses provide some information on a few other people involved in the butchery business in Sampford Peverell during the last 200 years, but often without much detail on where they lived or traded.

James Surridge

James Surridge was born in 1773, probably in Somerset. He married Martha Prickman in Wellington in March 1796. By 1797 he was working as a butcher in Sampford Peverell, and in that year took on John Radford as an apprentice. It is difficult to determine from which premises he carried on his trade, because he occupied more than one property and acquired additional premises over the next two decades. In 1815 he was named as one of the many tradespeople in Sampford Peverell who had loaned money to John Shuckburgh, but had not been repaid; John Shuckburgh was subsequently imprisoned for debt. By 1823 James rented "Morles", "Curham Meadow" and "part of Farrs" from John Bult, but he also owned "part of Butteridge", "Kerslakes", "Worth Orchard", "part of Canningtons & Rows", "Canal Grounds", "Saunders", and "Moor plot and Moor Meadows", most of which he also occupied[8].

In 1825, James ceased to occupy the properties that he had been renting from John Bult, one of which was "Morles", otherwise known as "Slee's Morrells". Part of this appears to have been "The Globe Inn", whilst another part continued as a butcher's, but was now occupied by another butcher, William Pine. So perhaps James Surridge gave up being a butcher at this time. He died in 1831 aged 58. There is more about William Pine in the section on 12 Lower Town ("Challis").

John Greenslade

John Greenslade, who lived in Higher Town, is the only butcher, other than Richard Shackell at Challis, listed on the 1841 Census. In the Tithe Apportionment of 1844 he is recorded as the occupier of part of the complex of buildings known as the Ghost House in Higher Town, in a building set back a little from the road. From 1845 he was also appointed to be one of the ten Parish Constables, a role which he held for the rest of his life. An 1847 newspaper report of a disturbance at the Globe Inn mentions John Greenslade and another of the Constables, William Taylor, the tailor. Apparently, in an earlier case, they expected money and suggested they would not assist the Globe's landlord again if they were not paid. The magistrate in this case "commented severely on the misconduct of the constables in the little money transaction already mentioned." He is not listed in White's Directory of 1850, so there may not have been a shop at his premises. In the 1851 census he is still living in Higher Town, but he died in 1853, aged 53.

John Greenslade's signature on 1852 petition
Courtesy of findmypast.co.uk

John Fisher

In the 1841, John Fisher is recorded as a farmer at Bubhays, Hemyock, but he moved to Sampford Peverell in about 1846. In 1847 he is listed on the Electoral Roll at Morrells Farm, which is the farm opposite the Globe Inn. It seems probable that he took over Morrell's Farm following the death of the previous farmer there, Richard Ponsford, and after Richard's widow, Mary, had moved across the road to Challis House. By the time of the next census, in 1851, 52 year-old John was firmly established at the 110 acre farm, with his wife Phoebe, daughter Elizabeth, a lodger and five servants, including 14 year old John Bowden, as butcher's apprentice. In 1856, John was described as "butcher and farmer; also licensed to let horses" [for hire][9]. In 1861, the census records John Fisher as a butcher - no longer a farmer - and his household had reduced a little to his wife Phoebe, two servants and a ploughboy.

After 1863, his name no longer appeared in the Electoral Roll for Sampford Peverell, because he had given up Morrells Farm and moved to another property of lower value, which did not qualify him to be listed as an elector. He already rented another property, known as 'Mount Stephen Oak', so it seems likely that he moved there[8]. His wife, Phoebe, died in 1866 in

Morrells Farm in 2018 Photo: Peter Bowers

Crediton (perhaps she had connections there), aged 63. John, however, remained in the village, and in the 1871 census he was recorded at 'Mount Stephen' in Lower Town; almost certainly the same as 'Mount Stephen Oak' and which today is called 'Mountain Oak'. By now he was 72, described as a butcher and farmer, but living there with just one servant. It is likely that he retired and moved away in about 1874, which is the last year that his name appeared in the Land Tax Returns.

Mountain Oak in 2018   Photo: Peter Bowers

Robert Jacobs

Robert Jacobs was born in Chatham, Kent, in 1816, but moved to Culmstock by 1840 where he married Elizabeth Haddon. In the following year, the census records his occupation as a butcher. At the time of the census in 1851 he was still in Culmstock, but by now working as a Grocer and Draper. From Culmstock the family moved to Willand in about 1854, where Robert became the licensee of the Halfway House Inn, as well as a butcher and farmer. A newspaper report dated 30 November 1860[10] announced that he was an insolvent debtor who was to appear in court in the following month for the first examination of his debts, estates and effects. The Halfway House Inn was then advertised[11] to be let from 21 March 1861 and the Jacobs family subsequently vacated the property and moved to Sampford

Peverell. Here the family, now comprised of Robert and Elizabeth and their seven children aged from 2 to 18, were recorded in the 1861 census as living in Higher Town, with Robert's occupation described as a butcher. Considering his situation as an insolvent debtor, it is most unlikely that he would have had the capital to set up a business of his own, so he was probably working for one of the other butchers in the village.

This is probably the same Robert Jacobs who was in court again in 1862, when he disputed the amount of a debt that he owed, part of which related to the charge for repairing a wagon. He was now described as 'being late of the Railway Hotel Uffculme' and his occupation as 'in the public house line'. It was explained to the court that Robert was bankrupt with eight children depending on him. He had sold all his goods and had been in 'most distressing circumstances'. The judge ruled that the full amount of the debt was due, but agreed that he would pay by instalments[12]. By 1866, Robert had returned to Culmstock, where he became a bailiff, a responsible position which required him to take possession of people's effects in circumstances similar to his own[13]. Although he remained as a bailiff for several more years, by the time of the 1881 census he had returned to being a butcher in Culmstock, as he had been 40 years previously. He died in 1882.

Tom Wensley

Tom Wensley first appears in Sampford Peverell listed as a butcher in Kelly's Directory of 1889, and subsequently on the 1891 Census, aged 59, described as "Butcher", living at "Kings" in Lower Town with his wife Sarah. He was born in Milverton in about 1836, married Sarah Morgan, from Holywell Lake, in 1862, and was a butter dealer in Hockworthy in 1881[14]. He probably arrived in the village in about 1884, when he was first listed as the occupier of Kings[8]. Soon after this he must have got into financial difficulties as he was named in the newspapers as insolvent in 1886, described as "Tom Wensley, general dealer, Sampford Peverell."[15] In November 1894 he appeared at Tiverton court: "Tom Wensley, butcher, Sampford Peverell, v George Downie. This was a claim of 14s 6d for meat." The case was adjourned and we don't know the outcome but it shows he was back in business as a butcher.[16]

The 1901 Census lists the couple still at Kings, where his occupation is given as "Butcher & Shopkeeper", so we know that he had a shop and wasn't just supplying meat to outlets elsewhere. Kings, or Kings House, was located between the "Hare & Hounds" (now "Coronation Cottages")

Lower Town, Kings in centre, circa 1950

and "Morrell's Farm"; the site is now occupied by a pair of semi-detached houses. Tom Wensley died in 1901, aged 62. His wife Sarah died in 1910, aged 77. They don't appear to have had any children.

Elizabeth Rolestone

In 1862 Elizabeth Ellen Glanvill(e), born in Broadclyst in 1841, married John Rolestone, born in Honiton in 1837. In the 1871 Census John is shown as the licensee of the Butcher's Arms, Mariansleigh, but by 1880 the family had moved to Sampford Peverell. He was described as a butcher of Sampford Peverell in a court case in which he was found guilty of stealing 89 cabbage plants from a neighbour who was a market gardener (Western Times, 13 April 1880). However, his occupation appears to have changed, because in the 1881 Census John is described as an agricultural labourer, Elizabeth as a housewife, and they are living at one of many properties identified as "Boobery Cottage". John died of pneumonia in 1886. At the time of the next Census, in 1891, Elizabeth - by now aged 50 - had moved to Pond Cottage, near Sampford Barton, where her occupation was described as "Pork Butcher".

In Gregory's directories for 1894 and 1897, she is listed as a "butcher of Higher Town'"(1894) and "butcher etc of Bidgoods" (1897). It was reported in the Western Times in March 1896 that "Elizabeth Ellen Rollestone, butcher, Sampford Peverell" was fined six shillings for having non-standard weights in her possession. In 1900, still living at Bidgoods, she married John Needes, the shoe-maker. They continued to live in Higher Town, but, as the 1901 census did not record an occupation for Elizabeth, perhaps she had given up working as a butcher.

Benjamin Hooper

Benjamin Hooper was born in 1849, the son of James Hooper, butcher and innkeeper at the Horse & Jockey in Burlescombe, and his wife Eliza[17]. In 1871, Benjamin was still at home working as an assistant innkeeper. He married Elizabeth Shere Dillon, of South Molton, in 1873, and was a butcher at "Ebear" (Westleigh) in 1881. He first appears on records for Sampford Peverell in the Electoral Roll for 1885, when he was occupying a property in Lower Town, known as "Kings Cottage". As Tom Wensley was also at Kings, perhaps he had come to work for him. Benjamin moved to Higher Town in 1888. In March that year he was sued for £12 for breach of warranty with respect to a pony: he and Henry Elworthy had agreed to swap ponies, and Elworthy said they agreed either could return a pony if not happy with it[18]. Elworthy found his new pony was slightly lame and wanted to swap it back, but Hooper refused, denying there had been any agreement to swap back, and later sold it for £7. Witnesses, including Joseph Goffin of the New Inn, suggested the problem should have been obvious to Elworthy. Eventually the jury found for Elworthy, but reduced the damages awarded from £12 to £4. In the 1891 Census he is living in Higher Town with Elizabeth and giving his occupation as "Butcher" but by 1901 he was a "Butcher's Assistant", suggesting that he was not in business on his own account; perhaps he was working for Tom Wensley or James Salter (Williams at Challis would seem to have quite enough help already!). When he appeared in court at Cullompton that year for using obscene language he was described as a 'slaughterman'. His defence was that "his wife was deaf and he had to shout", a statement which was greeted with laughter[19]. He was named in the Western Times again in March 1902 after a court appearance.

> At Cullompton Sessions yesterday, Benjamin Hooper, butcher, of Sampford Peverell, was summoned for the use of obscene language within hearing of the highway on March 7. P.C.Fewings said he heard defendant use most disgusting language towards his wife. Defendant said he was only speaking loud to his wife as she was hard of hearing.

He used no obscene words. He was angry because having the gout at the time. He wanted to go to bed, and his wife had not made the bed. There were previous convictions for like offences, and a fine of 10s inclusive was now imposed.

In 1911, Benjamin Hooper, now aged 61 and still with his wife in Higher Town, describes himself on the Census form as "Working Butcher (own account)", although the trade directories do not list him as having a shop. He was in the newspapers again in 1921, when he was again fined five shillings for using obscene language:

Defendant, who pleaded guilty, said when he got home no supper was ready, and as he had had nothing but a pint of cider since breakfast, he became angry. His wife was deaf, and he had to shout to her. P.C.Beavis said the bad language could be heard some distance from the house.[20]

The long-suffering Elizabeth died later that year, and Benjamin Hooper died in 1923.

Little Turberfield Farm Shop

With the closure of Arthur Wheeler's business in 1974 (see section on 12 Lower Town - Challis), the production and retailing of meat products appeared to have ended for good in Sampford Peverell, forcing residents to venture further afield - which many people had been doing for some years already. However, the advent of a Farm Shop on the road to the Tiverton Parkway railway station in 1980 provided the opportunity for customers to buy their weekend joint locally again. Further details can be found in Chapter 9 - Shops in 2020.

Chapter 4

Grocers and Drapers

Introduction

We may think of grocers' shops as selling food, and drapers' shops as selling material and haberdashery items, but although these might have been separate shops in large towns and cities, small towns and villages such as Sampford Peverell had general shops which sold a wide range of products. Such shops developed from the sixteenth century onwards as a result of increasing trade in foodstuffs grown, or goods made, outside the immediate locality or even abroad. Exotic products like spices, sugar, coffee, cocoa, dried fruit and tobacco were initially only available in towns, but demand quickly led to them becoming available in rural shops as well (Carole Shammas, chapter 8, see Bibliography). As an example, a list of the goods belonging to Uffculme shopkeeper Edmund Cole when he died in 1628, included cloth, linen,

'Mrs Tetterby Marketing' by Charles Green scanned by P Allingham on www.victorianweb.org

serge, stockings, tobacco, soap, candles, raisins, currants and sugar (from Uffculme Wills, see Bibliography). As time went on general shops added more items to their stock, such as sweets, cleaning products, medicines, items of clothing and household objects. Tea became hugely popular from the eighteenth century onwards, and tinned goods started to appear in the early nineteenth century, though the tins had to be hammered open - tin openers weren't invented until the 1850s! As our shopkeepers often gave their occupation as 'grocer and draper' we are covering all such shops in this one chapter.

9 Higher Town – Chorleys

In the bell-tower of St John the Baptist Church, mounted on a wall, is displayed a hand-painted wooden board which lists 13 properties in Sampford Peverell. The board is easily overlooked today, but its contents had considerable significance to the poor of this parish back in 1750, when it was created. Headed 'Donation of lands belonging to such poor of the Parish as do not receive any weekly relief' it sets out which properties had been donated by benefactors (whose names had been erased from memory by the passage of time), what rents were due on each, and consequently how much money should be available each year for distribution to the poor and needy who qualified under the terms of the charity that oversaw it. That charity, which had been in existence since the 17th century or earlier, was run voluntarily by up to 16 trustees (or 'feoffees' as they were known in earlier times), and was generally known as the 'Poor Lands Charity'.

Among this list of properties were four tenements (i.e. rented properties, each one capable of being occupied by more than one independent household), which were described as 'adjoining', and 'in the fore street situate near the Cross.' Their location has been determined from subsequent maps and documents as being in the row of cottages at the north-eastern end of Higher Town, from what is now Cross Hill up to, but probably excluding, Rose Cottage. The actual buildings on this site have changed considerably over time, as have the number of separate households and the purpose to which the buildings were put.

Hugh Isaac was named as one of the occupiers of these tenements on the 1750 list. Hugh, whose wife Elizabeth had passed away six years earlier, died in 1770. It is likely that within a few years, the tenancy was taken over by William Hellyer, who was baptised in Sampford Peverell in 1754, the son of George Hellyer. He married Elizabeth Upton at St Mary Major, Exeter in 1778 and the couple went on to have seven children who survived to adulthood: three boys and four girls. William's occupation was a staymaker (i.e. a maker of ladies' corsets, using whalebones or leather as the means of support) and shopkeeper. He was also a prominent Wesleyan Methodist in the parish, being one of the original trustees (of which his son William junior was another) of the Chapel, erected and opened in Higher Town in 1802.

From an inquiry into the Charity's lands carried out in 1820, we know that William senior already had two houses and a cottage, all of which were leased to him under 99 year leases (which would terminate upon the death of the last named of three persons selected by him) from the feoffees of the

Poor Lands Charity. Two of these leases had been due for renewal in about 1812, but were not put into effect until 1820, when the lives upon which the leases were determinable were stated[21]. For the first house, William named his three sons (William, John and George), and for the second he named three of his daughters (Sarah, Mary and Jane). Susanna, the fourth daughter, being married by this time, was excluded. This mechanism enabled William to pass on his houses and businesses to his children when he died. The remaining property, a cottage, was to be determined on the life of William Darch, whose name also appeared on the list of occupiers in 1750, and about whom there is more in the chapter on Shoes.

From the 1819 Rate Book we learn that William Hellyer (senior) paid rates on two shops, a house and a cottage. His three sons also had properties of their own, although all were under rental agreements with their owners. William junior's property was at 'Late Ballamy's', later to be known as the 'Ghost House' (see the chapter on Bakers). John had two properties: 'part of Ware's' and 'Heritage Meadow'. George had 'Royal Oak', which by that time was de-licensed as a public house and was used as a private residence. Like his father, George was also a Wesleyan Methodist; in 1817, when his occupation was described as 'Grocer', he applied for his house to be licensed as a meeting house for the Wesleyan Methodists. With the Methodist Chapel being only a few yards away from George's house, this act is difficult to explain. It has, however, been suggested[22] that there were problems with access to the Chapel at this time, which were only resolved three years later by William Hellyer (whether senior or junior we cannot now tell) purchasing an adjacent cottage on

The grocer

Child Land by Pietsch and Rictor on www.gutenberg.org

behalf of the trustees, with the view of demolishing it to provide a new point of access.

Documents from later in their lives tell us that William junior was a linen draper, John was a baker, and Mary and Jane were shopkeepers. We may infer that, at this time, all members of the family were quite well-off, and that the unmarried daughters were helping to run the two shops, whilst the sons were in business on their own account, probably selling some of their goods through their father's shops.

Between 1819 and 1828, a few changes in the family's property portfolio took place. George gave up the 'Royal Oak' to his brother John, and is not named as the occupier of any other property in the village - so he may have moved into his parents' house, or possibly moved away for a while. William junior gave up the Ghost House and moved into a much more modest cottage with a low rental value.

The reason for William junior's move becomes clear in a report in the Exeter and Plymouth Gazette of 11 November 1824: he was facing insolvency. Unlike the other debtors at the Insolvent Debtors Court hearing reported upon on that day, William junior was not discharged, but his case was adjourned until the next Circuit so that he could amend his schedule of accounts. There is no newspaper report about the next hearing, but the outcome was that he was committed to debtors' prison at the Gaol of St Thomas the Apostle in Exeter. An eye-witness report written by a visitor to this gaol a few years earlier had recorded the appalling conditions there[23].

By being committed to debtors' prison, William junior not only brought shame upon the family, but was also dependent upon them for whatever financial support they could provide. The gaol was privately owned, with board and lodging having to be paid for, whilst William would also have been attempting to reduce his debts. There can be little doubt that the Hellyer family's finances would have been stretched at this time. William senior died in 1828 at the age of 74, with his son William junior's financial difficulties still unresolved.

William junior was released from gaol by 1831, but the law at that time did not allow him to 'wipe the slate clean'. Instead, if a discharged debtor were to come by any property, his creditors were able to take possession of it. An advertisement in The Exeter and Plymouth Gazette of 30 July 1831 notified William the younger's creditors that he had, indeed, come into some funds through a marriage settlement made by his father-in-law (Henry Stevens, deceased) to William's wife Ann Stevens. The outcome of the meeting to discuss this is not reported, but we can presume that William junior did not prosper for the remainder of his life - he died four years later.

Following William senior's death in 1828, the future for his retail business was soon settled. In his will, he left all of his effects and estate to his unmarried daughters Mary and Jane, save for bequests to four of his other children, each of whom was to receive a copy of the British and Foreign Bible Society's edition of the Bible; perhaps this was one of the items that he stocked in his shop. His son George received nothing under the Will, but perhaps, as a practising Methodist, he already had a copy of this edition of the Bible, which his father was obviously keen to promote.

What appears to have been the main residence of William Hellyer senior, i.e. his house and two shops, was now in the names of Mary and Jane. From 1828, the Rate Books generally (but not consistently) refer to 'shop' in the singular, so it would seem that they only had need for one retail outlet. George acquired a separate property to live in, described as 'house and garden' in Higher Town, which he soon turned into a 'house and shop' the story of which is continued in the section on 14 Higher Town. William senior's other son, John, who was a baker living at 'Royal Oak', died in 1831. The remainder of this section follows the 'house and two shops' in Higher Town, leased from the feoffees of the Poor Lands Charity, starting with Mary and Jane Hellyer.

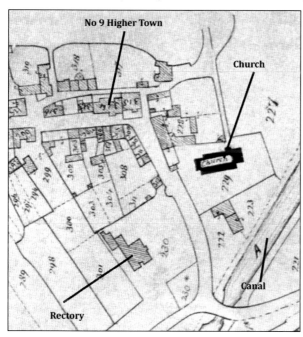

The 1841 census shows that Mary and Jane Hellyer were, indeed, shopkeepers and managed their premises with one live-in servant girl, who was actually their niece, Susan Knight. In the Tithe Map and Apportionment of 1844 we find that the location of Mary and Jane Hellier's house and shop was plot

1844 Tithe map, showing location of the Helliers' house and shop

Courtesy of Devon Archives & Local Studies, DHC DEX/4/a/TM/Sampford Peverell

number 314, which is now No. 9 Higher Town almost opposite George's house and shop. Mary and Jane did not occupy the same building that can be seen at No. 9 today, but a broader one (sometimes referred to as 'Chorleys') which filled the entire road frontage between what is now known as Cross Hill and Rose Cottage (11 Higher Town). It is not difficult to imagine that a property of this size could provide adaptable accommodation, in such a way that the former, and now unwanted, second shop could have been converted into living space.

In 1847, Jane died at the age of 53, leaving Mary to run the business on her own. White's Directory of 1850 lists Mary as a Grocer and Draper. Her brother George is also shown as such, but listed separately, confirming that they were each running their own business. The 1851 Census shows that Mary was still running the business with the aid of her niece Susan Knight, now aged 23 and a dressmaker, and a 14-year-old servant girl.

A court case reported in the Western Times on 25 March 1855 indicates that Mary had given up her shop business by then, although she was attempting to collect monies owing to her. 'The Plaintiff (*Mary Hellyer*) who formerly carried on the business of a shopkeeper at Sampford Peverell, sued the defendant (*William Parr*), a thatcher of Tiverton for £5. 2s. 2d., for shop goods'. His Honour gave judgement for virtually all of that sum in Mary's favour.

From about 1855, the House and shop were taken over by John Taylor, whose name first appears in Kelly's trade directory of 1856, as a draper and grocer. Mary's name is no longer listed, and it may be that she went to help her brother, now in his seventies, run his shop. Her story is continued in the section on 14 Higher Town.

John Taylor's life, just a year or two before he had moved to Sampford Peverell, had seemed settled as a farmer in Broadclyst. In the 1851 census, 40-year-old John had been married to Maria and they had 4 children. Living with them at the farm were two house servants: 13-year-old Caroline Ingersent and 18-year-old James Pyle. But tragedy struck in 1855, when Maria died. John seems to have acted quickly, moving to Sampford Peverell with his family and young female servant to take up his new career as a shopkeeper. Two years later, he married his servant, Caroline Ingersent, who had now reached the age of 18 or 19, and the couple had a son the next year.

The 1861 Census sees the new family settled in Higher Town, with John as shopkeeper and Caroline looking after three of John's children from his previous marriage (the eldest having moved away), and her own three-year-old son. Kelly's trade directory of 1866 informs us that John had added 'beer retailer' to his trade of grocer and draper. Thereafter, his health deteriorated and he died of tuberculosis in 1869 at the age of 58. Caroline continued to bring up the children and run the business in her sole name for a short while – she is listed in Morris' 1870 trade directory - but it was not long before she developed a relationship with a neighbouring shopkeeper by the name of Richard Southwood (see the chapter on Bakers). They married in the first quarter of 1871 and, in the Census of that year, are to be found living in Higher Town with three children: George (13), Elizabeth (7) and Mary (4), all of whom were the children of John Taylor. Although we cannot be certain, it would seem that the new family was living at Richard Southwood's house and shop known as Skinners (one of the properties on the site of 4 Higher Town) across the road from Chorleys (the name by which 9 Higher Town was sometimes known), and that the latter was left uninhabited.

The Land Tax Return of 1872 shows that Richard Southwood had taken over the lease for Chorleys from Caroline. It seems that the couple tried to combine their lines of business - Richard's bakery and Caroline's grocery - because Kelly's directory of 1873 describes him as 'grocer, baker and beer retailer'. However, they may have continued to operate the shop from Skinners for several more years until making the move to Chorleys, in order to make use of the bakehouse at the former. The Land Tax Returns show no entry for Chorleys between 1874 and 1879, so either it was left vacant or perhaps it was undergoing renovation.

The Western Times of 6 June 1878 contains the court report of a married woman, Maria Stephens, who carried a baby whilst stealing some copper coins from a till in Richard Southwood's shop, for which she was sent to prison for two weeks. Another report from the 17 September edition of the same newspaper shows that Richard also got into trouble. In this report he was described as a 'baker and innkeeper', although it is uncertain at which inn he was working (it may have been the New Inn, which also had a bakehouse and where the licensee, Joseph Goffin, worked as a tailor). He was summonsed for keeping his pig sties in a state injurious to health. Caroline, his wife, appeared on behalf of the defendant and said that most of the manure had been removed. Richard had to pay the Court's costs and comply with the notices that he had been sent.

In the 1881 census Richard, who was living with his wife Caroline, stepson George aged 23, and stepdaughter Mary aged 14, still described his occupation as baker and innkeeper, but by 1883 (according to Kelly's Directory) he had become a grocer and was no longer working as a baker.

By now, he had given up Skinners and had moved his family into Chorleys, from where he ran the grocer's shop for another two decades. His other property, Skinners, according to a 1904 report written to explain the property's omission from the Land Tax Return, 'had been void for many years and (the cottages) are in fact in ruins'.

A report in the Western Morning News of 7 July 1902 provides the reason for his grocery business coming to an end: the property was very badly damaged by fire, which may have started in the thatched roof of his cottage and spread to other buildings nearby. He was not insured, and lost almost everything. He died in the following year; Caroline having passed away 4 years previously.

In fact, the property had been so badly damaged that it had to be pulled down. Another building was erected on part of the same plot of land, which was named 'Paulett House' by its new occupier James Salter (see the chapter on Butchers).

11a Higher Town - Halls

11a Higher Town, known as 'Halls', is a private residence which dates back at least to the early 17th century. An indenture, or rental contract, dated 10 November 1653 seems to pertain to Halls. The contract is between John Lord Poulett, the owner of most of the properties in the village at the time, and "Maria Blakaller of Sampford Peverell in the County of Devon widowe". It concerns:

> all that messuage, dwelling house or tenement ... situate lying and bound within the Borowe of Sampford Peverell aforesaid, between the land sometime of Hugo Crosse now of George Hukely on the East parte, the streete or way there leadinge from Sampford Church towarde Uplomon on the South parte, a little lane there on the West parte, and one other Street or back lane there on the North parte.

Halls House and shop on left, circa 1903

The first mention we have of its being called 'Halls' is in the 1836-1840 Rate Book which lists it as being unoccupied. Soon after this, in the 1844 Tithe Apportionment, 'Halls house and garden' was owned by Thomas Broom Row, the trustees of Harriet Parkhouse, and Jane Francis. It was occupied by Prior Fry, a man of independent means (Prior was his name, not an ecclesiastical title) who was originally from Somerset, and who owned a number of properties in the village. He died in 1847, aged 83, and was buried in Sampford.

In 1851 it was still a private residence, but by 1861 'Halls Cottage' had come into commercial use when it was owned and occupied by Richard Jennings, who was both a Wesleyan schoolmaster and a glazier who was born in Sampford Peverell. His father, John Jennings, had also been a glazier, his brother William, who lived with them in Halls, was a painter and paper hanger, and his brother Joseph later became the postmaster (see the chapter on the Post Office). Richard Jennings was married to Elizabeth, and had two daughters, Bessie and Emma. In the 1870 trade directory, he is described as a "plumber, glazier, painter and paperhanger". Richard Jennings lived in Halls until the late 1870s, and probably used the extension on the side of the building as a workshop.

In, or shortly before, 1879, the Jennings family moved to Crediton, and 'Halls House' was taken over by Charles Nichols, a gentleman annuitant, whose son was a teacher. He put the house up for sale in late 1881, and the advert described it as a "convenient freehold dwelling-house, with offices adjoining, situated in Higher Town...The dwelling-house comprises dining and drawing-rooms, kitchens, 5 bedrooms, and all necessary conveniences." By 1883 the new owner and occupier was William Dunn, a boot and shoemaker. He was there until 1920, and he used part of the house and the area on the side as a shop and work area. The 1910 survey[2] gives this description of Halls: "Stone and cob plastered and slate cottage and garden. Ground Floor: Passage, Sitting room, Kitchen, brick built workshop, pantry. 1st Floor: 4 bedrooms. Garden with linhay and earth closet. Substantially repaired since 1909." Its market value was estimated at £100. William Dunn, known as 'Cocky' Dunn, we don't know why, had been a boot and shoe maker in Sampford Peverell since 1870, and there is a wonderful description of him in Denis Cluett's memoirs[35] around 1910, when William Dunn was in his seventies. It includes this:

> He worked in front of the window of his tiny workshop which opened onto the village street. He was a wizened little man and was always either hammering or sewing leather as if his life depended on the number of nails he could hammer in or the number of stitches he could make in a given time.

There is more about Cocky Dunn in the chapter on Shoes.

From 1920 onwards William and Lucy Snell occupied Halls Cottage. William was born in Halberton in October 1883, and married Lucy Knowles in 1912. They had two sons: Wilfred and Stanley. Wilfred died in 1929, at the age of 15. It was the Snells who converted the side workshop into a proper shop. In the trade directories in the 1920s it was described as a tobacconist's, but by 1930 it was a grocer's shop. In 1939[5] William was described as a general labourer, and Lucy as a 'shopkeeper, grocer and general unpaid domestic duties'. Their son Stanley was a 'weaver, woollen and worsted, textile factory', so he probably worked at Heathcoat's factory in Tiverton. It sounds as if the shop was mainly being run by Mrs Snell. William Snell died in 1940. We are not sure whether, or for how long, Lucy continued to run the shop, but she certainly continued to live in Halls House until her death in June 1955. After that, according to a former Sampford Peverell resident, Martin Reid, Cecil Court took over the shop.

The Courts were advertising it in the parish magazine in January 1957 as 'The Little Shop Top the Hill'. They were agents for Walls ice cream, Bradburys seeds, pink Aladdin paraffin, Hales cakes etc. They could also supply cakes for special occasions at short notice, "any size, decoration and wording to your requirements at 3/6 lb." In 1958 they were "the stores where less buys more" and were advertising their "Harris" bacon. The Courts were not there long, and the shop was taken over in late 1959 or early 1960 by Alan Alford.

Alan Alford renamed the shop 'Higher Town Stores' and was still advertising 'Harris' bacon in April 1960. Martin Reid recalls that Tony Alford (son of the shopkeeper) went to a private school in Jersey. From there, he sent a package to his father which, for the purpose of the Customs Declaration, he labelled 'Lambretta parts'. At the time Jersey was a duty free zone and there were strict import controls in place for items being sent from there to the mainland. The package cleared Customs without any

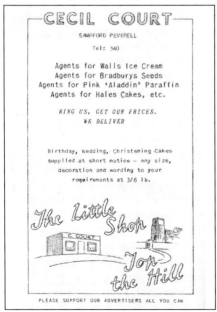

Parish magazine advertisement, January 1957

problems; inside were cigarettes, which his father was then able to sell for a substantial profit in his shop!

The Alfords can't have run the shop for long, because in 1961 it had been taken over by Owen and Patricia Wright. One of the Wrights' adverts in the parish magazine that year describes new products they have in stock:

> We have for a very nice (though, we admit, expensive) treat, SMOKED SALMON. Our range of cheeses now includes Edam, Port Salud (*sic*) (both mild), Wensleydale, Parmesan and Farmhouse, as well as those mentioned last month. If you are entertaining and want to give your friends something different and delicious - why not try a Chinese meal? NEW in the market is a sponge roll filled with jam and ice-cream. And for those alone or in a hurry for a man-sized dinner: FISH, CHIPS and PEAS.

In July 1961 they advertised "traditional cider, sparkling or still, sweet or dry, by bottle or barrel, as well as "Cydrax" (a sparkling apple juice) and a range of beers. Beer was still the theme in May 1963 when they were offering "Watney, Whitbread, Bass, Ind Coope, Tivvy, Courage, or whatever your special preference is from 9½d a half-pint" as well as various cordials. Moving on a few years, in February 1969 they had special offers on tea, Daz, and Domestos. They also mentioned that "we give GREEN SHIELD STAMPS on all purchases except cigarettes and spirits. EXTRA STAMPS on all biscuits and cakes for the next two weeks."[24]

Higher Town Stores, 1959   *Photo: Martin Reid*

We don't know exactly why or when, but the shop must have closed soon after this. Jeff Parsons, another local resident, remembers that by the time he moved to the village in 1970 the shop no longer existed. Owen Wright died in June 1971, but Patricia Wright continued to live in Halls with her daughter, Sara, and since then it has remained a private residence.

14 Higher Town - Cowlins

Adjacent to the Sampford Peverell Primary School railings, on the eastern side, stands a large fine house with double bow windows, which for at least 150 years was a prosperous retail business premises. The first definite mention of a shop in this building comes in the 1830 Rate Book, which describes it as a 'House and Shop', owned and occupied by George Hellyer (*sometimes written as Hellier*). George had been born and baptised in Sampford Peverell in 1784, the son of William and Elizabeth Hellyer (mentioned earlier in the section on 9 Higher Town). George married Anne Harwood of Halberton in 1817, whose health, it would seem, had been poor for many years. He wrote an endorsement, which was published in the Taunton Courier in 1821, praising medication in the form of tablets supplied by J Snook, Chemist and Druggist of Bridgwater saying that his wife had been suffering biliousness, stomach problems and dizziness from childhood but decided to try Snook's pills:

> After using only one small box, she obtained a relief the most extraordinary and unexpected. It is now six months since she experienced this singular benefit, and has since that time enjoyed a good degree of health. These facts are generally known in Sampford and its neighbourhood, and have been the means of rendering your Pills eminently popular.

As we saw in the section on 9 Higher Town, George's father, William, had two shops, numbers 9 and 14 Higher Town. After his father's death in 1828, George ran number 14 and his sisters Mary and Jane ran number 9. George continued to run his shop throughout the 1830s, but then his life was to change again. Despite the benefits of the medication, George's wife Anne died in 1840. He was re-married in the following year to Elizabeth Melhuish at St John the Baptist Church, Sampford Peverell, both parties being "of mature years". The 1841 Census, taken during the period when he was a widower, confirms that George was still a shopkeeper as well as a shop owner. He lived on the premises with three servants, who, one presumes, helped in the shop.

The Tithe Map and Apportionment of 1844 confirm the location of his 'house, garden etc', as plot number 302, on the eastern side of Royal Oak cottages, now 14 Higher Town. On Fair Day, 28th April 1845 'George Hellyer, draper etc' was mentioned in The Taunton Courier when a cow made her way up a flight of 15 stairs to the drawing room of his home but was subsequently persuaded to leave quietly, as described in this newspaper article.

> **SINGULAR ADVENTURE OF A COW.**—At the annual cattle fair, held at Sampford Peverell, on Monday last, April 28th, a cow entered the residence of Mr. George Hellyer, draper, &c., and *sans ceremonie* proceeded up stairs, (15 steps in number), and entered the drawing room, but not finding there suitable refreshment, she walked to the window and quietly gazed on the astonished spectators below, she then quietly withdrew from that appartment and was proceeding to the sleeping rooms, when her intrusion into the abodes of Morpheus was prevented by his sentinels who had stationed themselves at the doors. To the great satisfaction of the household, she was then prevailed upon by gentle treatment quietly to withdraw, walking down stairs and leaving the house but little the worse for her visit.

Taunton Courier, 7 May 1845   Image reproduced with kind permission of The British Newspaper Archive
(www.britishnewspaperarchive.co.uk). Image ©THE BRITISH LIBRARY BOARD, ALL RIGHTS RESERVED.

White's Directory dated 1850 lists both George Hellyer and his sister Mary as a grocer and draper, but they are listed separately, confirming that they were running separate businesses. Their sister Jane had died in 1847, at the age of 53. In 1851[3] George was living with his second wife Elizabeth, known as Bessie, and an unmarried niece, Elizabeth Hellyer, who was a servant.

Over the next few years, the nature of George's business changed a little, as Kelly's 1856 directory shows that besides his Grocery and Drapery business, he was also an agent for the London Union Assurance company. In Billing's Directory of 1857 George Hellyer is shown as a Shop Keeper and General Dealer. Mary Hellyer is no longer listed, because her business had been taken over by John Taylor in about 1855. Perhaps Mary and George had decided that running two shops was too much for them - by this time George was in his seventies - and Mary had moved in to help George in his shop.

The cow at George Hellyer's residence

Illustration by Denis Holwill

George died in 1860, leaving the house and shop to his sister Mary[8]. Mary lived in the property with George's widow Elizabeth, described as the head of the household, and they ran the business between them: Elizabeth aged 74 and Mary aged 71, both giving their occupations as grocer and draper, helped by a servant[17].

In November 1863 Elizabeth sued John Williams, a carpenter from Bampton, for the sum of 10 shillings and 2 pence – a debt unpaid by his daughter, a servant in the employ of the local doctor. She had purchased candles, raisins and currants etc for her father plus a dress for herself. The judge decreed that the daughter was responsible for paying for her dress and that if details of the grocery purchases were forthcoming he would award Elizabeth the full amount.

Soon after this, it would appear that Elizabeth and Mary gave up running the shop. They are no longer listed in directories of commercial premises, although a newcomer's name appears for the first time in Kelly's 1866 Directory: Charles Vickery as a grocer, draper and photographer. Elizabeth died in 1867 and it is probable that Mary had decided to retire by then. The Land Tax Return completed in May 1866 shows that although Mary was still the owner of the House and Shop, it was occupied by Charles Vickery. Charles was born in Sampford Peverell in 1841, and in 1866 he married Laura Southwood, the daughter of Richard Southwood, the baker.

By 1868, Charles Vickery had become the owner and had let the premises to Thomas Kerslake. Charles' name and occupation, however, still appeared in Morris' trade directory for 1870, with Thomas Kerslake shown as a lime burner. Whatever Charles Vickery's involvement in the shop had been, his tenure there was short-lived. In the 1871 census Charles had moved to Bishopsteignton, where he traded as a draper and grocer, and the

Higher Town premises are listed as 'grocer's shop unoccupied'. In the same census, Thomas Kerslake was a lime burner, living at Kiln House (now Hill Kiln). This situation was not to last long, as evidenced by the 1872 Land Tax Return which records Thomas Kerslake as both proprietor and occupier of the Higher Town house and shop. Kelly's 1873 directory shows that, for a while, he was continuing to ply his trade as a lime burner, whilst also being a grocer and draper - a most unusual combination - so it was probably his wife who was running the shop.

Thomas had decided upon this change of career somewhat late in life (he was aged 57 in 1873), probably because of his wife's family connections. In 1837, he had married Jane Knight, a staymaker, just one month prior to the birth of their first daughter, Lydia, and they proceeded to have at least another 5 children. Jane Knight was a granddaughter of William Hellyer, an early owner of the shop, and niece to George Hellyer and his sister Mary Hellyer, the previous owners. During the 1870s, Thomas' trade was described variously in directories - sometimes as grocer and draper, at others also as a lime burner, so it would appear that he had not given up his previous trade of lime burning and his wife probably took a key role in running the shop.

By 1881 Thomas Kerslake, his wife Jane and unmarried daughters Susanna (born 1853) and Elizabeth (born 1854) were living at the grocer's and draper's shop, which was, for the first time, listed as 'Cowlins, Higher Town'[25]. Thomas was still working as a lime burner, whilst Jane and the two daughters ran the shop. Their son John had taken over as lime burner at Kiln House, living there with his wife Charlotte and a growing family.

After both Thomas and Jane died in 1887 the shop passed down to yet another generation of Hellyer descendants: Susanna, the elder daughter, took over the business, running it with her sister Elizabeth. Susanna's name, together with her trade of grocer, appears in directories until 1894, when she married Samuel Holloway, who was 11 years her junior.

Samuel Holloway, a baker and corn merchant, was a native of Halberton and the son of William Holloway, miller and baker. He married Eliza Bowbeer in 1885 and the couple had one daughter, Millford, the following year. However, Eliza died in 1891, leaving Samuel to look after his young daughter. Three years later, he married Susanna Kerslake in Sampford Peverell and moved into Cowlins with her, Millford and Susanna's sister Elizabeth. Samuel extended the range of goods offered by the shop with the addition of his bakery products, and soon took over running it. In 1895 Samuel was described as being a shopkeeper in Sampford Peverell in two newspaper articles:

One found him in Court being sued for trespass in Halberton, a situation that also involved his mother who claimed damages for assault from the land owner following a 'scrimmage' (*i.e. scuffle or brawl*) with the landowner over a right-of-way. The other article concerned a summons for delivering bread without taking scales to weigh the bread should this be required. Mr Holloway replied in his defence that the boy he employed was starting on another short journey to deliver groceries and five loaves and forgot to put them in. He was fined 5 shillings but no conviction was recorded against him. Photos show that the shop was now known as "Holloways".

In 1896 Susanna gave birth to Samuel Cromwell Holloway and the 1901 Census shows Samuel with Susanna, Millford aged 14 and Samuel Cromwell aged 5 living at the shop, with the adults carrying on the business of Baker, Grocer and Draper. Elizabeth had moved out, and was living alone in a 2-roomed property in Torquay, working in a shop.

The 1910 Survey[2] provides a description of the premises at that time: "Stone, cob and slate house with Baker and Grocers Shop. Ground Floor - double fronted shop, private entrance, sitting room, kitchen pantry, bakehouse with loft over, coach entrance, store and tiled stable (old) and leanto washhouse".

In the 1911 census, Samuel's occupations were unchanged but he had been joined by his 25-year-old daughter Millford, who assisted her parents. Samuel continued to be listed in various directories as Baker and Grocer until 1914. In that year another newspaper article noted that Samuel Holloway addressed a Sunday evening open-air meeting of the Free Churches in Halberton, held on the banks of the canal. Another brief article announced the marriage of Millford, Samuel's daughter from his first marriage, to Albert Dinham, who was employed as a Clerk for R.S.Norrish, owner and manager of the Creamery in Chains Road (which will be the subject of a chapter in another book).

Holloway's shop, circa 1900

Samuel senior died in 1916 aged 52, and it would seem that the remaining members of the family gave up running the shop shortly after that. His son, Samuel Cromwell Holloway, served in the Royal Army Medical Corps during the First World War, where he contracted malaria, and was discharged in 1919. He achieved notoriety in the High Court in the following year when he was sued for Breach of Promise, having jilted his fiancée by sending her a letter saying that he had married someone else. The jury awarded the aggrieved party, Miss Gladys Minnie Evans, £100 damages - a very considerable sum.

Gregory's Directory for 1920 records that Susanna Holloway was living at another address in Higher Town along with her step-daughter Millford and Millford's husband Albert Dinham. However, Susanna continued to own the shop, as evidenced in the Land Tax Returns for the same year.

After Samuel Holloway's death in 1916 William Chidgey took over the bakery side, operating it in conjunction with his other bakery in Halberton. He was called up for War service in May 1917, after losing his appeal against conscription at a Military Tribunal: the Tribunal decided that one bakery was sufficient in Sampford Peverell, despite the increased demand for bread during the War. William's mother, Laura Chidgey, may have been helping him at this time, but it is not until the Electoral Roll of 1918 that we have confirmation that she was living in the village - and probably at the Higher Town shop - as she was described as a grocer and draper in the trade directories.

After the War, William returned to his main business in Halberton, but continued to supply the Sampford Peverell shop with bread from there. He married Alice Wright in 1919 and they moved into Hill Head, in Halberton[26]. He was soon in trouble with the law, as reported in the Exeter and Plymouth Gazette of 17 September 1919, when he was fined £1 for "selling bread that had not been made for at least 12 hours". Wheat was scarce during the First World War, and in 1917 the Government tried to discourage people from buying bread by making it illegal for bakers to sell bread that was less than 12 hours old. The rule had not been rescinded by 1919 but people wanted fresh bread again, and Mr Chidgey said other bakers were selling it, so he had to as well.

By 1929 Laura Chidgey had left Sampford Peverell and moved to Halberton to live with William and Alice in Hill Head. Alice died in 1935 but William and his mother were still there in 1939, with William described as a 'bread and cake maker, grocer', and his mother carrying out unpaid domestic duties[5]. With Cowlins vacated, the time had come for a new occupant with a different trade.

Frank Kingdom's name first appears in Sampford Peverell's Electoral Roll of 1928 and he is listed in the 1930 edition of Kelly's Directory as a tailor. Born in 1898, he originated from Halberton and was one of four brothers, all tailors, as was their father. He married Elsie Cory in 1927 in Holsworthy and decided to set up a tailoring business on his own account in the old Holloway's shop which he rented from Susannah Holloway. The couple had one daughter, Joan. In 1937 Susannah Holloway died, so Frank and Elsie were able to buy the shop, and it was then that they expanded into a variety of goods.

Looking at the property as it is today, the bay window nearest to the school playground was their sitting room; the front door was in the same position as now; to the left of it there were two more bay windows, and then the tailor's window, which was where the garage door is currently situated. Joan recalled that there were two cottages next door which jutted out into the road; Mrs Dunn lived in one and Gladys Holley lived in the other. These two cottages originally formed The Royal Oak pub, but were demolished in, or soon after, 1961, to make space for a school playground.

At that time there were no mains utilities in the village and sometimes Frank would sit in the kitchen in the evenings working by the light of an 'Aladdin' paraffin lamp, especially if he had a rushed order to complete.

Cowlins in 2018   *Photo: Peter Bowers*

Water was drawn from the pump in Boobery or by the Barton. This was Joan's job when she came home from the Grammar School. Despite his tailoring work and haberdashery sales, overseen by Elsie, it would seem that Frank may have had difficulties making ends meet, as he was also a postman delivering mail from Mr Goffin's Post Office which was then situated next to the canal bridge.

For some years Frank worked alone until John Maynard, brother of Len Maynard and Victor who were the village bakers (see separate chapter on Bakers), asked if Mr Kingdom would consider taking him on as an apprentice. Frank replied that he wouldn't be able to pay much but John was happy to work for very little in order to learn a trade. After a while John became a promising tailor and, as everyone else did, referred to Mr Kingdom as 'Tailor' Kingdom. When Joan took piano lessons she would practise her scales in the house and this led John Maynard to comment that he would dearly love to be able to play the piano. 'Tailor' Kingdom said that he'd see how things went, but might see his way to paying for piano lessons for him. John was able to begin his lessons and astounded everyone by having a natural aptitude and soon outstripping Joan. 'Tailor' Kingdom set John on his musical career and he became a well-respected organist and composer. He taught at a private school in Coulsdon, Surrey, and collaborated on compositions with the poet Cecily Taylor, but died in 1985 at the age of 60.

On the other side of the Higher Town road, set in Back Street behind the London Inn and Halls, stood three thatched cottages. Joan, at home from school because of illness, remembered watching workmen remove the thatched roofs and replace them with slate - most likely as a belated safety measure following a devastating fire of three neighbouring cottages which stood just a few feet away on the opposite side of the road from the school and which were burnt to the ground in 1939. 'Tailor' Kingdom had joined the people helping to remove goods and furniture from the three cottages as the fire took hold. The tenants were Mrs Cornish, Mr & Miss Thomas (from the bakery) and the Cork family. Mrs Cornish had been away from home that day and on her return 'Tailor' Kingdom was pleased to tell her that most of her furniture had been rescued from the blaze. Far from being relieved that her possessions had been rescued, Mrs Cornish merely expressed the sentiment "I hope it hasn't been scratched!" Frank felt rather aggrieved by her lack of appreciation.

The shop consisted of counters forming a 'U' shape from which Mrs Kingdom sold underwear, trousers, socks, stockings, jumpers, cardigans and, at the time of Bampton Fair, raincoats. Apparently it always rained on Bampton Fair and Mrs Kingdom knew a good business opportunity when she saw one. People travelling to Bampton passed her shop so she made a point of buying in a quantity of raincoats, all of which got sold. Joan helped in the shop during school holidays and as a teenager went to the warehouses in Exeter to buy stock, but Joan had no interest in taking over the shop, preferring instead to become secretary to the headmaster of Heathcoat School in Tiverton, where she remained until she married. Frank and Elsie Kingdom sold the shop in 1965 and retired to the New Inn (by that time, a private house) further up Higher Town.

The new owner of the shop was a Pole named Jan Muzyka. He had married Pamela Carpenter in 1953 and the couple moved from Tonbridge in Kent to Sampford Peverell to take over 'Kingdom's' bringing four daughters with them. A fifth was born in 1968.

In October 1965 Jan Muzyka's first advertisement appeared in the Parish Magazine listing ladies', men's and children's wear, wool, fancy goods and clothing alterations, describing his premises as 'late Kingdom's.' By June 1969 the couple had become agents for Moss Bros, Swift Dry Cleaners and Crown and Sanderson wallpaper and by 1971 the shop carried a wide range of surprisingly modern garments. Jeff Parsons, a recently arrived villager, decided to take his wife Jenny to the local dance held at Green Headlands (a hotel on the corner of Whitnage Road and Lower Town, since demolished) and, in desperate need of a new tie, went to see Mr Muzyka from whom he was delighted to be able to purchase one of the very fashionable wide 'kipper' ties.

In the January 1972 edition of the Parish News "The Village Shop", as it was now known, was offering 'ladies', men's, and childrens' wear, groceries, cigarettes, fruit, vegetables, toys, wool, fancy goods and also ladies' and men's bespoke tailoring. However, despite their best efforts, the business became less and less viable and the Muzykas had to advertise a Closing Down Sale in June 1972. A "Note of Farewell" appeared in the Parish Magazine of August 1972. After at least 150 years as a shop, serving the needs of the residents, Cowlins became a private dwelling.

```
Advertisements
          "The Village Shop"
        (J.F. & P.I.M.R. MUZYKA)
Ladies', Men's and Children's Wear, Wools,
          Fancy Goods, etc.
            ALSO TAILORING
          Men's & Ladies'
    Alterations and Repairs undertaken.
14 Higher Town, Sampford.  (late Kingdom's)
```

Parish magazine advertisement, October 1965

21 Higher Town – London House

21 Higher Town, also known as London House, is an old building which is clearly marked on the 1796 map and probably dates to a period long before then. We know that in 1844[27] it was occupied by Henry Martin, who was described in the 1841 census as a shopkeeper living with his sister, Sylvia Martin, a servant. The property belonged to the Curwood family, but Henry Martin had been renting it since 1830, and his parents, Thomas and Mary Martin, had rented it before him from 1822 onwards[28]. It was a prime location for a shop, so might well have been one in their day as well. Henry Martin was born in Sampford Peverell in 1789, lived and worked here, later moved to Halberton, and was buried back in Sampford Peverell in 1857. Very little else is known about him, although he is mentioned in a newspaper report, when a brass pan was stolen from his garden in September 1830. The thief, William Warren, was given a harsh sentence: 4 months' imprisonment with hard labour, to include 4 weeks of solitary confinement[29].

Some time between 1844 and 1851 Henry Martin's nephew, Richard Harris, took over the premises and continued to run a shop there. He signed a petition in April 1852 as a "Draper etc" and was described in various other sources as a grocer and draper. He was also manager of the Bible Christian chapel located further up Higher Town, acting as preacher for this religious denomination. During Richard Harris' tenancy the property was owned by Mark Saunders, who

Horatio Sparkes, a draper by George Cruickshank
from www.victorianweb.org

remained as owner when Catherine Burrough took over the tenancy in 1863, from where she also sold groceries and drapery. An advert placed by her in the Tiverton Gazette in September 1863, describing the shop as 'late Harris's', announced:

> The reception of a Choice lot of GROCERIES of all descriptions, including several lots of Teas of superior fragrance, Coffees and Spices; Mats, Brushes, Earthenware, Glass, etc. CB also invites an inspection of the Drapery department which is now replete with choice Dress Goods, suitable for the coming season, comprising Poplinettes, new Lustres, Alpaca, Knickerbocker, Winseys, new Fancy Skirtings, and Ladies' and Gents' Ties, Collars and Setts in plain and sewed Muslin, Hats and Caps of every description, Plain and Fancy Handkerchiefs, Hair Netts, Hosiery and Gloves, Crinolines, Umbrellas, Sheets, Blankets, Flannels, Serges, Prints, Calicoes, etc etc at low prices, well worth an inspection. CB hopes by strict attention to business to merit and receive a share of public patronage.

By 1868 Catherine Burrough had moved to Exeter where she was advertising a similar establishment, and the shop was taken over by Edward Sherry. This must have happened in mid 1867 as a newspaper article in September of that year reported that Edward Sherry, general dealer, was fined for having light weights, and his defence was that he had only just taken over the business and assumed the weights were correct. Some significant changes took place in 1869 / 1870 after Edward Sherry's arrival: the property was given the name 'London House'; Edward Sherry became both the owner and occupier, thereby ending Mark Saunders' interest in the premises; and Edward broadened the range of goods available. In addition to being a grocer and draper, he was an ironmonger and an agent for W & A Gilbey, wine and spirit merchants. We know he also sold footwear, as a case was brought against a woman accused of defrauding him of a pair of boots, but she was acquitted as the identity of the thief could not be proved. Mr Sherry's tenure was short-lived, as he died aged 36 in 1875, to be succeeded briefly by his widow, to whom his wine licence was transferred.

21 Higher Town was then sold to John Hellier, and a new tenant shopkeeper was found: Mrs Elizabeth Morgan. By 1881 Elizabeth Morgan, who came from Culmstock, was living in London House with her two adult daughters, Eliza and Emily, and 14-year-old son, Thomas. An older son, James, had joined them by 1891, but Eliza died at the age of 33. Mrs Morgan sold the same range of items as Edward Sherry. Later, after her death in 1896 when she was succeeded in the business by her sons, James and Thomas

Morgan, the additional lines of 'boot warehousemen and general stores' were added. We know that these 'general stores' included stationery, because they supplied the National School across the road with paper[30].

In 1899 another major change occurred when the property's name was altered again, this time to 'London Inn', under a new owner, Francis Snow. Two tenants followed in rapid succession: Mr Chappell and Ernest Thorne. During the latter's tenure in 1901 Robert Parr, the thatcher, was accused of being drunk in the pub. Various witnesses were called including "T Morgan, grocer (who had previously helped his mother run the shop)", so Thomas Morgan had presumably moved to a different shop. In May of the following year Ernest Thorne, now described as a grocer rather than a public house licensee, made another appearance at Cullompton Sessions, on this occasion being summonsed for keeping a dog without a licence, for which he was found guilty and fined £1. Later in 1902 the London Inn was sold on to a Taunton-based brewery, Hanbury and Cotching. Intriguingly, the new occupier, George H Preece, continued to sell groceries from the establishment (perhaps due to the loss of the Southwood/Morgan grocer's shop which had been destroyed by fire) whilst also running it as licensed premises. However, in March 1903, his licence was not renewed by the Licensing Authorities.

Perhaps Sampford Peverell could not support a fourth public house at that time. Although Mr Preece remained as occupier of London House until about 1906 when Samuel Hellyer took over, there is no evidence that the licence was regained. In 1909, the building became vacant and it then came to the attention of the Church Institute. No other records of this Institute have been found, but we can surmise that its purpose was to provide a meeting place for Church members outside of the Church building. Reverend P C Rossiter, who was the Parish Curate at the time, offered to buy the empty premises for use by the Institute, and a caretaker, Mr Knight, was duly appointed. The Land Tax Returns for the period during which the Church Institute was the occupier of the property continue to show its name as 'London Inn', although we think it unlikely that the Church Institute would have wished to retain any association with a licensed public house! The 1910 survey[2] calls it a "Men's Club" and describes the property as follows:

> House – Cob & slate containing :- large room (shop), small room, kitchen, sitting room, 4 bedrooms. In yard there is a cob shed with galvanized Iron roof. Water supply obtained from own well by pump. The premises are old and in bad repair.

Not long after the purchase of 'London Inn' for use by the Church Institute had been completed, Reverend Rossiter died. Although the premises were still occupied by the Institute until 1913 under three subsequent owners (Mrs Rossiter, W J Venton and P Walters), perhaps its days had been numbered without the driving force of the benevolent Minister.

A new purpose for the building was found in 1913 as the Village Post Office, under postmistress Mrs Rosa Martha Jennings, who moved the Post Office business from Bridge House, where it had been located for a considerable time (see the chapter on the Post Office). Two years later, she was succeeded as postmistress by Maud Taylor, who had been a Post Office assistant for many years. Maud Taylor did not manage the business well, and was accused of embezzlement (see the Post Office chapter). She was committed to trial in August 1917, and found guilty. A new postmaster, Frederick Goffin, was appointed in December 1917, and he moved the Post Office back to its former site at Bridge House. No new tenants were found for No. 21, which had now reverted to its earlier name of 'London House,' and it remained vacant for the next 12 years, whilst still in the ownership of Mr Walters.

Yet another use was found for the premises on 1 January 1929 when the property was bought by Victor Eli Parkhouse, who re-opened it as Parkhouse's shoe shop. There is more about the shoe shop in the chapter on Shoes. During the Second World War both English and American servicemen were billeted in the house – some upstairs with the Parkhouses and some in the cellar, which had its own outside entrance. Victor Parkhouse died in 1953, but his widow, Rosalie, kept the business running and by 1961 the shop was also dealing in other household goods. Rosalie, who had subsequently married Walter Redstone, became the new postmistress for the village in 1963, and the Post Office business moved from Lower Town back into London House. In addition to functioning as the Post Office, the shop now stocked stationery and birthday cards, Pyrex, wellingtons, slippers and plimsolls. The Redstones retired in 1966 and the Post Office was run by the Averys until 1978, the Fergusons until 1990, and the Learys until 1999 when Peter and Philippa Flatters took over. There is more about the postal services in the chapter on the Post Office.

Each new occupier made some adjustments to the range of products that was available, with footwear eventually diminishing to just flip-flops. However, as other shops closed elsewhere in the village, so the potential to offer other items increased. In this way, the Learys sold sweets, toys and gifts, and the Flatters took on the sale of fresh bread, milk and newspapers (although they did not make deliveries). When Peter and Philippa Flatters first arrived, business was quiet and Peter could manage the shop and Post Office on his own. Philippa told us that with the additional custom, they had to open for longer hours and employ staff to help. Profits quadrupled because, by 2001, it was the only shop in the village; being always busy, it became the hub of the community.

The shop sold groceries, bread, milk, stationery, cards, toys, puzzles and cigarettes. They even displayed house sale advertisments for a Tiverton estate agent. Philippa enjoyed dealing with the local suppliers such as Gundenhams Dairy, Crusty Cottage Bakery, Gamblin eggs, and many others. Most of the groceries were purchased from Bookers, a wholesale 'cash and carry' business.

One day, a local off-duty policeman was collecting his children from school when he spotted that, unnoticed by Philippa or Peter, a notorious petty criminal was shoplifting. He challenged him and inside his coat in various pockets were packets of biscuits, tins and bottles. After being relieved of his booty, he was sent off with a stern warning and he could be heard cursing and muttering all the way up the street.

London House, 2018   *Photo: Peter Bowers*

At that time, the shop had an awning over the front. One wet day, one of the teachers from the Primary School opposite nipped over to collect the milk for the teachers' coffee. When passing beneath the canopy, which had collected a huge volume of water, it collapsed and the poor teacher got soaked!

In 2007 the Flatters sold the Post Office to Mike van Bussel, but the following year the Spar shop opened in Lower Town and business started to decline. The shop closed for the last time in January 2010, and soon afterwards the Spar shop took over the Post Office business. Since 2010 London House has been a private residence.

24 Higher Town – Coombe Cottage

William Hooper Daniel was born in St Austell, Cornwall in 1802, and subsequently moved to Exeter. In 1833 he married Elizabeth King from Sampford Peverell in the parish church. The couple must have stayed in Sampford Peverell after the marriage, because their four children were born here - Richard, Harriet, John and William. They were not, however, baptised in St John the Baptist Church. In 1838 the family occupied a house and garden (otherwise described as 2 cottages and gardens) called Coombe at 24 Higher Town. This has since been demolished to provide the access road from Higher Town to Blackdown View. In the 1841 census William is described as a shopkeeper, so we can assume that he ran his shop from these premises. He was a friend and supporter of the Bible Christians, and it is probably no coincidence that the family had chosen to live just a few yards away from the functioning Bible Christian chapel in Higher Town. In 1842, he acted as a trustee for a new Bible Christian chapel which opened in St Andrew Street, Tiverton and he may well have been one of the contributors to the £200 cost of acquiring it. The document naming him as a trustee also gave his occupation as a grocer of Sampford Peverell, so we know the nature of his business. Two years later his wife Elizabeth died at the age of 42 and, left with a shop to run and four young children to bring up, William lost no time in re-marrying: later that year he married Susanna Thorne in North Devon.

Now aged about 42 years, Susanna Thorne had been born into a devout Christian family in Shebbear, North Devon. As a teenager, she had been among the very first members of the Bible Christian Church, the initial assembly of which took place in her family home at Lake Farm, Shebbear in 1816. One of Susanna's brothers, James, went on to become the leader of the Bible Christian Church from 1829 until his death in 1872. Another brother, John, became a missionary for the Church in Canada, whilst Samuel, her third brother, set up a printing press at the farm from which all the Church's publicity material and hymn books were produced. One of the features of the Bible Christian movement was the inclusion of female preachers, and it is probable that Susanna and her only sister Mary toured around the Bible Christian chapels of Devon and Cornwall (the Church's stronghold) speaking at the local meetings. It is therefore likely that she would already have been well acquainted with William Hooper Daniel, which would account for their brief period of courtship.

The new family remained in Sampford Peverell for at least another year, during which time William was a Parish Constable[43], but then moved to Halberton to run a grocery and drug shop there. In the 1851 census, William Hooper Daniel is described as a 'general shopkeeper' living with his wife, Susanna, and his four children.

Susanna died in the following year. Subsequently, William became ill and took on the services of a live-in nurse, Elizabeth Frost. It was on 9 October 1854 that a most unpleasant incident occurred: William's son John, now aged 15, attempted to poison him. The facts of the case came out at John's trial, which was reported in the Exeter and Plymouth Gazette on 24 March 1855. Elizabeth Frost had been preparing some rice for William to which John added some white powder when she wasn't looking. On spotting the powder, she tasted it and determined on account of its bitterness that it was neither salt nor flour as John had claimed. She informed her master who summoned the constable, and John was arrested. It transpired that, three days earlier, John had wished his father in 'hell fires' because his father had struck him for telling a lie. John had tried to take revenge by acquiring some 'white precipitate' from his father's drug and grocery shop. White precipitate is a compound of mercury which has medicinal purposes when used externally for skin problems, but which is poisonous if swallowed. John was found guilty, and although both the Jury and prosecution asked for leniency due to his youth, the Judge decided that he should make an example of him. He was given four years penal servitude.

Six weeks after this incident and four months before John's trial, William Hooper Daniel died. There is no further mention of the remaining Daniel children in Halberton, whose lives must have been devastated by the events of the previous three years.

25 and 27 Lower Town – Barum House

25 Lower Town is an old cottage which can be seen on maps going back to 1796, and which may be much older. We can tell from the 1844 Tithe Map and Apportionment that it was then owned by the trustees of Jane Francis, and occupied by John Tapper. John Tapper was a 60-year-old harness maker and was living there with two young children, perhaps his grandchildren[31]. It is not clear who was living in the cottage in the 1850s but we can follow its history after that. In the early 1860s it was described as 'cottages' owned by Jane Francis and occupied by "Baker and others". This was probably 70-year-old Richard Baker, an agricultural labourer, and his wife Ann, 74[17]. They were followed as occupants by "Jennings and others" in 1867, Lovell in 1868, and Lovell and Jennings in 1869, by which point the cottages had become the property of a Mr Tremlett[8]. From the 1887 Ordnance Survey map it appears that the building may have been a pair of semi-detached dwellings at one time, so perhaps the Lovells were in one half and the Jennings family in the other.

This particular Jennings was William who was born in Sampford Peverell in 1840, the son of John Jennings, a glazier. He was the younger brother of Richard Jennings, a glazier and Methodist schoolmaster who lived in Halls, Higher Town, and of Joseph Jennings, who ran the Post Office for many years. William was variously described as a painter, glazier and paper hanger during his long career. He married Ellen Vickery, daughter of a local blacksmith, in 1865, which is probably when he first moved into the cottage in Lower Town. Before that he had been living with his brother, Richard, in Halls. In 1871 William and his wife Ellen were in Lower

Town with their 3-year-old daughter, Lilley, and in 1873 William Jennings became the owner of the cottage. The 1878 Harrod's trade directory includes William Jennings as a painter and plumber, but it also lists his wife who is described as a grocer and draper: they had a shop in the cottage, which can be seen in this photo, taken some years later.

By 1881 they had another two children, Arthur and Charles (two other children had died young), and Mrs Ellen Jennings was described

Jennings' old shop on left, circa 1900

as a draper and grocer. In trade directories over the next thirty years she is regularly listed as either draper, grocer, fancy goods dealer, or some combination of those three. Their daughter Lilley, a dressmaker, married Edwin Karslake on 25th August 1892 and moved to Barnstaple. Their elder son, Arthur, a carpenter, moved to Stogumber between 1891 and 1901 and married a local girl there on 31st March 1901. Charles, their youngest child, moved to Taunton and was working there as a journeyman carpenter in 1901. On 18th May 1907 he married Emily Louisa Davey in Taunton and they moved back to Sampford Peverell.

Charles' marriage in 1907, perhaps coupled with a wish to expand the business, may have prompted the next development. The family decided to build a brand new house and shop in the garden to the east of the cottage, fronting the road. The 1910 survey[2] describes the plot as follows: "Lower Town. Site of house and shop, 8 perches 4 yards, occ. C Jennings. Small plot of land formerly part of garden of ref no 74 and now the site of a brick and tile house and shop erected since 1909. Site only valued. Enjoys a right of way over ref no 74." Property number 74 was the original cottage and shop next door and is described thus: "Lower Town. House and garden. Owner and occupier Wm Jennings. Cob and thatch cottage and garden part orchard. Contains GF Room was shop, sitting room, kitchen, workshop, washhouse. 1st Floor 3 bedrooms. Garden with store and GF EC. Old. Fair

Jennings' new shop in 1911, at the time of the coronation of King George V

repair." EC stood for Earth Closet – an outside toilet. Once the new shop was open, in what is now 27 Lower Town, they closed the shop in the old cottage and since then it has been purely residential.

In the 1911 census Charles, now a cabinet maker and photographer, named his new property as Barum House. Barum is the old name for Barnstaple and was perhaps named as such because his sister, Lilley, and her family lived in Barnstaple. It had six rooms, as did the old cottage next door where his parents lived. Ellen Jennings was still described as 'Shopkeeper general store" which suggests that it was she who was initially running the new shop. Charles and Emily had a daughter, Eileen, who was born in June 1912. William Jennings died on 22nd April 1918 leaving his money to his sons Arthur, now a joiner, and Charles now a general shopkeeper, indicating that Charles had taken over the store, selling groceries and fancy goods.

Denis Cluett, looking back to the period just before and during the First World War[35], remembers Charles Jennings as being "a slightly eccentric man", and proceeds to give a comprehensive description of his business – as seen through the eyes of a young boy:

> Charles' shop was always known as the Paper Shop, since it was he who had the village paper-round. In addition to the papers and periodicals

Jennings' old and new shops, circa 1910s

he sold sweets, fish-hooks, fishing lines, catapult elastic, penknives, sheets of transfers which we used to decorate the backs of our hands and, in their due season, fireworks, tinsel and Christmas cards.

Not surprisingly, he tells us:

This was my favourite shop and, when I could read, it was here that I spent most of the few pennies which came my way. I used to save up to buy the then well-known boys' papers, the "Magnet" and the "Gem" - these were school stories. Others were small novelettes, dealing with the adventures of famous detectives – Sexton Blake and Nelson Lee, with their respective young assistants, Tinker and Nipper. Another favourite amongst these small paperbacks was the Buffalo Bill Library...

Jennings' shop, circa 1920s

Thanks to Denis Cluett's recollections, we have a very rounded picture of Charles Jennings and his character:

I think most of the children loved his shop, not least because [he] was very soft-hearted, and by telling him a hard-luck story we could often persuade him to sell us something for a halfpenny which should have cost a penny.

and it would seem that he was quite a character. Denis mentions his trick of riding a bicycle backwards (see the chapter on Newsagents) and:

In addition to his activities engendered by the paper round and shop, Charles was also the village photographer and from time to time was called into service to produce photographs of wedding groups or newly-born children. Once a year he gave a magic lantern show in the chapel for the children and as there were no such things as the cinema, radio or television, this was regarded as quite an event. The show was exactly the same every year, as Charles possessed only one set of slides – Queen Victoria's funeral; nevertheless, we always thoroughly enjoyed it.

It is possible that the photos of Barum House which we have included in this book were taken by Charles Jennings. We know from trade directories that Charles Jennings remained trading at Barum House until 1933, when he sold the business to William ("Bill") Upham. We can only speculate on the reasons for his doing so; his mother Ellen had died, at the age of 89, in 1934, and maybe his "soft" heart never was in retailing, because in 1939[6] we find him working as an Electrical Engineer, Plumber and House Decorator, living at "The Cottage" - next door to Barum House – which he must have inherited from his mother. He shared the cottage with his daughter Eileen, a Ledger Clerk at Norrish's Creamery. Perhaps, also, the health of his wife Emily was a contributory factor – she died in the summer of 1935, aged 53.

When Bill Upham acquired the retail business Charles Jennings retained The Cottage, and lived there until he sold it to Dan Channon from Clyst Honiton in February 1940. It was here that "Red" and Glenys Thomas lodged briefly in 1947/48 while refurbishments were carried out to their shop "Challis Stores". Glenys recalled that toilet and washing facilities were extremely primitive, necessitating the use of a privy at the bottom of the garden and a visit to friendly neighbours or the public baths in Tiverton when they wanted a bath. At the time that the Thomas family were there, water had to be drawn from a well in the garden of Barum House, to which The Cottage had a right of way. Later, the property was connected to the mains water supply, and in 1966 Bill Upham made application for the right of way to be rescinded; shortly afterwards he bought the right of way, and the piece of land associated with it, for £100.

Bill Upham, known by many as 'Banana Bill', was born in Halberton in 1901, but he had family in Sampford Peverell. His aunt, Elizabeth Upham, married John Kerslake from Sampford and lived here from around 1900. Bill had many relations in the village, including his cousin Frederick Kerslake who ran a coal merchant's business in Lower Town. Bill had owned two shops in Tiverton by the Heathcoat's factory main gate until he and his wife Emily moved

Upham's shop, circa 1950s

Let..

U P H A M S

Supply you as they have done for 25 years with
Groceries, Fruit and Vegetables,
Confectionery & Ices,
Cakes & Sliced Bread daily
"Aladdin Paraffin"

TEL: SAMPFORD PEVERELL 286

ORDERS DELIVERED
NEAR AND FAR

AGENTS FOR "THE WELFARE FOODS"

*Parish magazine advertisement,
December 1957*

to Sampford Peverell when he bought Barum House. Their son Allan was two at the time and their daughter Pat had not yet been born. Allan was six years older than Pat, joined the Navy and had little connection with Sampford afterwards. The following five paragraphs are compiled from Pat's memories.

Her first memory of working in the shop was sitting at the kitchen table and counting out coupons from ration books and sorting them out for her father. During and after the Second World War certain basic commodities had to be rationed because of their scarcity. They could be obtained only on production of the ration book so that the appropriate coupon could be cut out or crossed off. No coupon – no food!

When Pat was 12 or 13 she rode her bike on fortnightly rounds to collect orders for her father to deliver in his car. Bill had two rounds: the first was Stag Mill, Uplowman, Whitnage and West Pitt; the second was Halberton, Ash Thomas and the surrounding farms. The orders were for greengroceries, general groceries and especially for paraffin as many country houses had no electricity and used oil lamps. The paraffin was delivered to the shop by a tanker which filled a large tank in the barn situated to the left of the house. From this Bill would fill a large container in his car, and later his van, with the required amount for the orders he had received. The recipients would fill their containers directly from Bill's van.

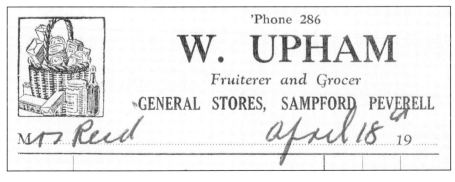

Upham's billhead, 1950s   *Courtesy of Martin Reid*

The shop was run mainly by Mr and Mrs Upham but they also used other people to help in the shop and the house. Joyce Herford was both nanny and cleaner. Ella Webber (née Williams) cleaned and helped generally in the house. Mrs Hookway helped in the shop as did Mr Gwinnell (Ruth Sharland's father).

When she was small Pat had a baby-sitter called Alice Pengelly. Whenever someone entered the shop wearing a red hat, Alice would always say "Red hat and no drawers" in front of Pat but not so that the customer could hear. One day in Church, which she had to attend regularly, Pat saw Mrs Anne Church, wife of Colonel Church, the Church Warden, wearing a red hat and shouted out, "Red hat and no drawers" much to the consternation of all around.

Pat lived at Barum House with Bill and Emily until she married Arthur Simmons in 1959 and moved to Tiverton. In later years her mother was often unwell and Pat frequently had to drive back from Tiverton to manage the shop. Bill was often unwell too, but it was not until he sold the shop to Ken Knowles in 1966 that he was diagnosed as having ulcers. When operated on it was discovered he was riddled with cancer.

Ken Knowles shared the following memories of Barum House with us. He came from Twickenham where he had been a policeman. Because he disliked the new shift system which meant he seldom saw his children, he followed the example of a colleague, who had resigned and bought a shop in Shebbear. Ken consulted a Devon-based estate agent and eventually chose Barum House. He bought the shop from Bill Upham who claimed he was so involved in village matters that he had little time for the shop. His deteriorating health must also have had a great influence on his decision. The idea had been that Ken's wife Rita would look after the shop while Ken updated the decor. Unfortunately she contracted cancer and had to spend much time in and out of hospital until she was cleared, so Ken had to look after the shop. He employed Bett Alford to help in the shop and with the deliveries.

Ken had a contract with the Midland Bank under which his dining room was used for two hours every Friday for local business people to pay in their proceeds and conduct other bank business. This came to an end in 1972 when the family had an urgent reason to be away one Friday. Midland Bank tried to hold Ken to his contract but he was adamant. He never heard from them again so Midland Bank ceased trading in the village.

When Ken was trading in the village it was still normal practice for local shops to provide a delivery service. Customers could call at the shop with

Parish magazine advertisement, January 1970

an order for, perhaps, a week's supply of groceries and other items, which Ken would deliver in his van - usually at a pre-arranged time. Customers would normally pay on delivery, but there was a high level of trust in small communities like Sampford, and Ken remembered an occasion when a customer in Boobery was leaving the house in a hurry when he arrived with her week's groceries; she shouted to him that the back door was unlocked and he would find her purse in the kitchen drawer!

Paraffin was still used, as many homes still had no electricity and lit their houses with oil lamps. Like some of his predecessors Ken kept a large tank of paraffin in his lean-to garage, which had been Bill Upham's barn. Customers brought their own cans for filling or had it delivered. Customers were good at paying even though some bills had to be left until the following week for payment. As the years passed Ken found keeping up with the invoices becoming more difficult. He used to get his daughter Jenny (who later married Stan Holley) to come in occasionally to catch up with the paperwork. Even so, some customers would ask for their bills week after week and have to wait sometimes for months before being able to pay.

The family had long played a game where one looked for car registration numbers of 1, then 2, then 3 and so on. Having come from London in the 60's, they found this was easier in Devon as there were fewer cars and they more frequently had lower numbers. It became a family habit to notice car numbers, which was particularly useful on one occasion. At lunchtimes the shop did not need to be shut while the family ate their meal as a bell on the door announced the arrival of a customer. However it was possible for someone entering to stop the bell from ringing by reaching up and holding it . One day Rita heard a noise in the shop while they were eating but had heard no bell. She went out and saw a man getting into a car and asked if he wanted anything but he drove away quickly. Only then did she notice the till drawer was open and the notes missing. Ken rang 999 and reported the theft. When asked for a description of the car, Rita was able to quote the registration number of the car because of their family game. The village bobby, P.C. Sid Wilson, caught the thief at Lamb Hill, near Uffculme, and found the stolen money in his sock.

Barum House was at that time the village paper shop and employed five boys to deliver the papers – there is more about this in the chapter on Newsagents. At that time, children were expected to help in the business. This often entailed rising early and delivering papers if a paper boy was ill, or helping with deliveries, often before school as well as after school. Each Saturday Jenny, aged 13 – 15, became the family cook as Saturdays were always busy days in the shop.

In 1975 Ken sold the shop to Ron Holland and his son. They very soon sold it on to Mike and Mavis Gee in 1977. By the time the Gees took over, the business had become somewhat run down and sold only "newspapers and a few odds and ends". They renamed the business "M & M Gee", enlarged the retail space into the garage (where previous owners had stored paraffin) and added a small sitting/dining room at the rear. The Gees built up the business adding groceries, fruit and vegetables and fresh-baked bread and cakes from Cullompton. When Dave and Joyce Wright ceased trading at Sampford Stores (see the section on Challis House and Challis Cottage), opposite the Merriemeade, Mike and Mavis added an off-licence. The business flourished and so did their social life, both becoming important members of the newly formed Sampford Peverell Tennis Club.

Then came the A361 Link Road, providing a fast route from the M5 to Barnstaple. Trade from outside reduced considerably as all through traffic drove down the link road and no longer entered the village. Previously the summer trade had helped them through the winter. To increase income Mike took on the school meal delivery service: he collected metal canisters of hot food from Willand School and delivered them to Sampford Peverell and Uplowman Primary Schools each lunch time.

HOLLANDS STORES

Grocers
and
Newsagents

● *PERSONAL SERVICE AND FREE GROCERY DELIVERY*

● *GREEN SHIELD STAMPS ON ALL PURCHASES*

Telephone
SAMPFORD PEVERELL 820540

Parish magazine advertisement, January 1976

Mavis and Michael Gee
GROCERS & NEWSAGENTS
Barum House, Lower Town, Sampford Peverell.   Telephone 820540

Stockists for   Choice Fruit and Vegetables, Chemist's
Culm Vale Bakery Bread and Cakes   Sundries, Paperbacks, Paraffin, etc.

PERSONAL SERVICE & FREE GROCERY DELIVERY

Parish magazine advertisement, January 1978

In 1978, when very deep snow stopped the milkman from reaching the village, the local dairy delivered directly to the shop, thus easing a difficult time for the inhabitants of Sampford. However the pull of supermarkets in Tiverton meant fewer customers came to Barum House and the Gees eventually sold up to the Sweetman family in 1984. According to an interview with Gill Sweetman, she and her husband Robert bought the business because they wanted to bring up their two children, Jenny aged 11 and James aged 9, in Devon rather than in the Home Counties as they felt it would be a better way of life for them. They chose Barum House after looking round Devon because the accommodation was ideal as they had Gill's mother living with them at the time and because the location was easy for family and friends to get back and forth to Henley-on-Thames, which is from where the Sweetmans originated.

The accommodation in the property was rather run down when they bought it so they spent a lot of money putting it right. The flat roof extension over the kitchen leaked like a sieve so they had that taken off and, before the builder could replace it, there were some terrible storms and the family spent several days and nights in the kitchen with lots of buckets and saucepans catching water. All this happened about two weeks after they had moved in. In those days there were many power cuts at frequent intervals, so their first impression of Sampford Peverell was not the best.

However, the family quickly settled into the life of the community; Robert played for the village cricket team and they made many good friends in the village. Gill comes back once a year to visit them. One thing they found strange was that when people came in to buy cheese they insisted it be cut in a special way: people wanted a perfect cube, which was not easy when cutting from a whole round cheese!

According to Gill the reason they left the village was that poor book-keeping caused them to lose a considerable amount of money, so they sold up while they could still raise enough to buy another property. They lasted only for two years and sold on to Jill and Chris Gabbey in 1986.

The Gabbeys came from London. They wanted to move for two reasons: Jill's elderly father lived alone in Cornwall and she wanted to keep an eye on him as he had had some unfortunate experiences with corrupt tradesmen; Jill and Chris's son Mathew was approaching school age and they did not agree with some of the very advanced ideas being forced onto London schools. They were looking for a business much nearer Cornwall and found Barum House, which was a suitable size and had a garden big enough for Mathew to play in. The size was important because Jill's father had by then sold his house in Cornwall and needed to move in with them.

The business had been run down, so they had a bakery built in, cooked their own meats and sold local milk. They had paper rounds in the surrounding villages out as far as Huntsham and made deliveries on a Friday evening to some of the older folk in the village. Chris remembers clearly delivering a box of groceries to Mrs Church, wife of Colonel Church, the Church Warden, and skidding across the hallway as it was so highly polished and slippery. He also found on one occasion that Leonard Perry, a somewhat eccentric old gentleman, who always directed traffic where Boobery meets Whitnage Road even if there was only one car, directed Chris into Boobery as usual, but by the time he had finished his deliveries and reached the other end of the road, there was Mr Perry once more directing him out of Boobery into Higher Town.

Barum House in 2018   *Photo: Peter Bowers*

They no longer sold paraffin as all houses in Sampford used electricity, but the original paraffin tank still exists. The original barn and later lean-to garage have now been incorporated into the living accommodation.

A necessary part of their equipment was a large chest freezer. After noticing a frail, small, elderly lady standing almost on her head as she rummaged in the deep freezer, Chris started checking each night to see that no-one had fallen in during the day! Like previous occupants, they did good business selling draught sherry from a cask. Customers brought their own bottles for filling and inevitably some drips fell onto the shelf below. When the bakery was being installed, they had to move the casks and found that, over years, the drips had worn through the paint and made a hole in the metal shelf. What price villagers' stomachs?

Jill and Chris's best times were when the last part of Fairfield and the whole of Coot Hide were being built. The builders would descend on Barum House at lunch-time to buy pasties and other savouries from their bakery. After that the business started to decline. Safeway's supermarket in Tiverton started to run a free bus on Saturday mornings to take prospective customers from outlying villages to do their shopping. This of course drew more customers away from the Gabbeys. The garage opposite Barum House was also feeling the pinch so they expanded their business to take in most of the goods already sold by Chris and Jill: fruit and vegetables and general groceries. There was not enough trade for one grocer in the village let alone two. To make matters worse the garage stopped letting their customers have monthly accounts, so people went elsewhere for their petrol. This took away the casual customer who had been used to visiting the shop after calling at the garage. Enough was enough, so they decided not to throw good money after bad and they closed the business in 1999. The competing garage closed soon after.

Jill Gabbey had always cooked for the shop and found another outlet by supplying food for the passengers of the horse drawn barge in Tiverton. She heard of another cooking opportunity at the Masonic Lodge in Uffculme, started there in 1999 almost as soon as the shop closed, and was later recommended to other Lodges in the area. Jill now, in 2018, cooks principally for the Lodge in Uffculme but occasionally caters for other events in the area. Her business is known as 'Barum Foods' and much of her cooking is done in the kitchen of Barum House, thus ensuring that business continues to be based there over 100 years after it was built.

8, 10 and 12 Lower Town – the 'Challis' buildings

Bordering the pavement and standing side by side in Lower Town today are three conjoined buildings of very different styles: the first, called 'Challis', a three storey Victorian house with bay windows on the ground floor, the second, 'Challis House', a double-fronted, sash-windowed house with an elegant Georgian doorway, and the third, 'Challis Cottage', a lower, long and narrow cottage from an earlier age. The casual observer would be forgiven for thinking that, throughout their long existence, they had always been dwelling-houses. In fact, they have all been used in the retail trade at some time during the 19th and 20th centuries, although no outward vestige of this past now remains.

The Tithe Map of 1844 provides us with a little more information about their origins. At that time, the predecessors of the properties that we now know as 'Challis' and 'Challis House' occupied one plot of land, and what is now 'Challis Cottage' another. Only the first two of these had 'Challis' in their names. The third property (now 'Challis Cottage') was shown in the Tithe Apportionment to have been occupied by a smallholder/farmer, who rented a few fields around the outskirts of the village.

The name 'Challis' was derived from 'Shallis': a Samuel Shallis, yeoman, was required to pay tax on an unnamed property until he died in 1762[8].

The Challis buildings, 2019   *Photo: Peter Bowers*

After he died, the property became known as 'late Shallises', and then later still, just 'Shallis'. It appears that within a decade of his death, new owners had built the new Georgian property adjacent to the original home, hence creating a second dwelling upon the one plot of land. From then on, the names of those who occupied both dwellings can be tracked through to the 1844 Tithe Apportionment list. By the 1860s, the property name 'Shallis' had evolved into 'Challis', by which name they are known to this day.

The following narrative tracks the development of the properties now known as 'Challis House' and (from towards the end of the 19th century) 'Challis Cottage'. The story of 'Challis' is to be found in the chapter on Butchers.

Challis House and Challis Cottage

The earliest reference we have to a shop on these premises is in an advertisement in the Western Times on 21st February 1846, when the building was owned by Mr Quick. The property was large and adapted for use both as a shop 'with two extensive windows' and as a dwelling house. At that time, a tenant was being sought for the property for a 7 year term. In the following year, the property was put up for sale by auction. In this advertisement (Western Times, 27 March 1847) additional information is supplied: the dwelling house was occupied by Mrs Mary Ponsford, and the 'spacious shop in front (*was*) well adapted for a grocer, draper, or any other business requiring room'. Mary was the widow of Richard Ponsford (otherwise 'Pounsford'), who had died in 1843, aged 53, and who had been the farmer at Morrell's Farm, also in the centre of Sampford Peverell village. Having been described as a housewife in the 1841 census, and as the occupier - although incorrectly named as 'Mary Poundsfield' - of Morrell's Farm in the 1844 Tithe Apportionment, it would appear that Mary moved across the road to Challis House to take up the seven year tenancy. Whether or not Mary was involved in running the shop is unclear. In 1851 she was living in Higher Town with her 19 year old daughter Grace, and working as

SAMPFORD PEVERELL, Devon.

TO be LET, for a Term of Seven Years, by Tender, from Lady-day, 1846, a neat
DWELLING HOUSE AND SHOP,
(With two extensive Windows,) in the centre of the lower town of Sampford Village.

The Dwelling-house contains a Parlour, Kitchen, Back Kitchen, Cellars, and seven Bed-rooms, with a small Courtlage at the back.

Also, TWO new-built COTTAGES, with an Acre of Walled Garden, (either together or separately,) situate in Ashford Moor, in the Parish of Sampford Peverell aforesaid.

Sampford Village is within ten minutes' walk, and Ashford Moor within five, of the Great Western Railway.

For viewing the respective Premises, apply to Mr. Quick, the Occupier and Owner.

Tenders to be sent to Mr. Baskerville, of Halberton, on or before the 16th day of March next.

Dated February 16th, 1846.

Western Times, 21 February 1846. Image reproduced with kind permission of The British Newspaper Archive (www.britishnewspaperarchive.co.uk). Image ©THE BRITISH LIBRARY BOARD, ALL RIGHTS RESERVED.

a seamstress, so it is improbable that she completed the full seven year tenure of Challis House.

The 1851 Census shows the business at Challis House to be occupied by Charlotte Creed, aged 54 and described as a grocer, apparently living there alone, although her son Joseph, a millwright, is living next door with his wife Mary. Charlotte was the widow of Thomas Creed, who occupied Sampford Mill in 1841 and died in 1847. It is probable that, at about this time, Challis House was provided with a second front door, which can be seen in photographs from the early 1900s, but was subsequently bricked up. Consequently, Charlotte was probably sharing the living space in Challis House with her son and daughter-in-law. The second access from the street enabled the house to be occupied by two different tenants, each tenant having space for a shop in one of the front rooms, presumably each shop having one of the two 'extensive windows'. Further indications of this arrangement come in the 1861 census, where it would appear that one part of the premises is occupied by the Creeds' shop, whilst the other part is occupied by William Taylor, a tailor and sub- postmaster.

With regard to the portion occupied by the Creeds, Charlotte relinquished control of the shop to her daughter Maryann (or Mary Ann) at some time before 1857. Charlotte continued to live at Challis House, no doubt helping her unmarried daughter out with the business from time to time, although the 1861 census records that Charlotte took on a new occupation as a schoolmistress. By 1871 Charlotte is described as a 75-year-old pauper, still living with her daughter but almost certainly at a different property in Lower Town. That same census describes Mary Ann as a shopkeeper, so she may have moved her business to another premises. Following her mother's example, she gave up being a shopkeeper and by 1881 had become a schoolmistress. She remained in the village, 10 years later being a shirt seamstress, and she died in 1897 aged 81.

The other portion of Challis House, which was occupied by 78-year-old William Taylor, became a Post Office[17] . He died later that year and the Post Office was taken over by Joseph Jennings who had previously run a shop in Higher Town. Joseph was helped by his wife, Martha, and Martha's niece Rosa who lived with them. There is more about the Post Office side of the business in another chapter. As well as running the Post Office, the 1866 trade directory describes him as being a "grocer and draper, coal and salt dealer." It is probably at around this time that Mary Ann Creed moved out, and the premises reverted to being in sole occupancy once more. However, the additional door to the street remained, now serving as the public entrance to the shop. By 1873 the shop was being run by a newcomer to the village, Federick Taudevin, as reported in The Exeter and Plymouth Gazette on 21 March 1873, which highlights how desperately poor many rural families were at that time:

> Maria Stevens, Sampford Peverell, a dejected-looking person with infant in arms, was charged with stealing on the 5th three buns value 3d from the counter in Mr Frederick Taudevin's shop. Prosecutor saw defendant at a little distance from his shop. He asked if she had purchased buns from any shop that morning and she answered the negative. He saw the buns under her shawl. She admitted the offence and begged forgiveness. The police heard of the matter, hence the present charge. Accused admitted the offence, and said in extenuation she did it as she had nothing to give her children to eat. The husband said he worked at the quarries at Sampford Peverell, but was almost blind, having received his injury whilst in the 39th Regiment, but had only served four years and some days and had no pension. His wages were 1s per day and the parish allowed him 2s per week and two loaves. He had a wife and six children to maintain out of it. He begged that his wife might be forgiven this time and thought it would be a warning to her for the future. The bench said they should be glad to accede to the request but for a former conviction appearing against the defendant. The sentence, therefore, would be seven days' imprisonment with hard labour.

Sampford Fair outside Taudevin's shop, circa 1900

An advertisement in the Exeter and Plymouth Gazette in October 1884 informs us that the freehold interest in two properties between the high road and the Canal, which from their further descriptions appear to be 'Challis' and 'Challis House', were auctioned on behalf of trustees under the will of Richard Gunn, deceased. At that time, Challis House was described as a 'modern dwelling house, with shop and stores, yard and large garden... in the occupation of Mr Taudevin, grocer and draper'. A notice in the Western Times a week later, on 21st October 1884, shows that it was bought by the occupier, Frederick Taudevin, for £275, after some spirited bidding.

Frederick (baptised 'Frederic') William Taudevin was born in St Peter Port, Guernsey, the son of Joseph and Mary Taudevin, in 1846. He came over to the mainland at some time after 1861 (when he was a "Draper's Assistant" in St Peter Port) and married a Cornish girl, Caroline Lanyon, in 1871.

"Taudevin's" became established as the Lower Town grocer's shop for over seventy years, run by two generations of the family. The shop itself was situated in Challis House, although it would appear that the neighbouring building of Challis Cottage may have been used for storage of stock

Frederick Taudevin, from Western Times, 29 January 1909.
Image reproduced with kind permission of The British Newspaper Archive (www.britishnewspaperarchive.co.uk). Image ©THE BRITISH LIBRARY BOARD, ALL RIGHTS RESERVED.

Taudevin's shop, circa 1910

from around the time that the Taudevin's business opened. The business did well, and another branch was opened in Uplowman. Frederick Taudevin died unexpectedly in 1909, aged 63. The Western Times reported his death on 29th January 1909 of which the following is an extract: 'he was a staunch advocate of Liberal principles and took an active interest in Nonconformist matters, being one of the local preachers on the Wesleyan circuit plan. He has been a member of the Parish Council for many years and his death will be a great loss to that body.'

Thereafter, his widow Caroline took over the premises and the business as "Proprietress" with her son, also Frederick William, as "Manager" and her daughter Ethel Mary described as "Shop Assistant". Caroline died in 1925, aged 81.

The 1910 Survey[2] described the property thus:

> Stone, cob, stucco and slate house and shop with some old cob ground floor (*i.e. single storey*) buildings adjoining. Contains on ground floor a double fronted shop (Grocer) partly extended into the old parlour, private entrance, sitting room, kitchen, larder. First floor 4 bedrooms, 1 small room. Attic over. Outside, stone and slate washouse. Adjoining shop, cob and ground floor store with loft over and leanto shed.

Denis Cluett[35] recalls that "...Taudevin's Store was run by a brother and sister with the aid of a middle-aged woman assistant whom Taudevin later married". This was Beatrice Ruth White, whom Frederick William Taudevin junior married in Gloucester in 1914. Denis Cluett goes on to describe the shop, as he remembers it:

> They sold groceries and haberdashery. Taudevin was a good businessman and ran a delivery service to outlying farms and hamlets in the parish. He used to go around on his bicycle on Wednesdays taking orders which he delivered by horse-drawn van on Saturdays. From his shop one could buy almost anything from lard and cheese to paraffin and candles. He always wore a long white apron, tied around the waist and reaching to his boot-tops. His aprons were never hemmed at the bottom and consequently always had a frayed edge.

The First World War brought tragedy to the Taudevin family. In November 1917 the Western Times reports the death of Wilfred Taudevin, second son of Frederick William senior :

> Mrs F. W. Taudevin, "Challis House" Sampford Peverell, has received news that her second son, Pte. Wilfred Taudevin, Somerset Regt. of Andover Hants, has been killed in action. Pte. Taudevin was 38 years old and leaves a widow but no family. The widowed mother has another son serving in India.

An article in the Exeter and Plymouth Gazette in September 1920 records that Frederick had to appear before Cullompton Petty Sessions to answer for an infringement of the pricing regulations. At that time, the Ministry of Food set maximum prices at which foodstuffs could be sold. A Ministry inspector had visited Taudevin's shop and had enquired about the price of a tin of salmon. He was told 1s 0½d, which was 3½d more than the permitted maximum. After claiming that the price quoted was a guess, and therefore an honest mistake, Frederick pleaded guilty and was fined £1.

The business remained in the Taudevin family until 1937 when Federick offered the business premises for sale at auction. Described in the Exeter and Plymouth Gazette advertisement of 16 July 1937 as "an important business premises, whereon for over 60 years a Grocer's business has been carried on", it was subsequently sold.

By 1939 the premises and business had been taken over by Henry and Winifred Skinner[6]. They were a young couple, aged 24 and 23 respectively, and Henry was described as a Grocer, General Dealer and Confectioner (cake maker). Winifred carried out domestic duties. They did not stay long, because in the early 1940s a middle-aged couple, Charles Robert Spring and his wife, bought the premises and continued the business there under the name of "Challis Stores". After the War, early in 1947, Edmund Levi

Challis Stores (mainly in Challis House, but now also in Challis Cottage), early 1940s

Thomas (known to everyone as "Red", on account of his ginger hair) and his wife Glenys arrived from Cardiff to rent and run the shop.

"Red" Thomas had been born in Tonypandy, as had Glenys, and spent most of the Second World War as a POW in Germany. When the Thomases arrived, the shop consisted of Challis Cottage (then only single-storey with a loft above, and used mostly for storage) and the adjacent front room at Challis House. The living accommodation for themselves and their young baby (Bruce) in Challis Cottage was very basic; the storeroom was their living-room and they slept in the loft and cooked on a primus stove.

Soon Mrs Spring, who was still living in Challis House, decided she wanted to remove the shop from her front room, so she had the loft of Challis Cottage converted and extended upwards into living accommodation. This enabled the shop to be operated wholly from Challis Cottage. During the conversion work at Challis Cottage the Thomas family moved into temporary accommodation – first with George Quick in Coronation Cottages, and later with Mrs Shannon at 25 Lower Town, where they used a privy at the bottom of the garden and had to go to friendly neighbours or the public baths in St Andrew Street in Tiverton for bathing. Challis House became a private dwelling, occupied by Mr and Mrs Spring until November 1950, when they sold the house and most of their belongings and moved away; it has remained as a private house ever since then. However, Mr Spring retained ownership of Challis Cottage and continued to lease the premises to Mr Thomas.

Once the Thomases were properly installed above the shop, the business prospered. To help him, Red took on two sisters, Margaret and Sheila Radford, and he bought a vehicle for deliveries which was driven at first by Glenys – at one time travelling with her baby son in a grocery box behind the driving seat. In 1955 Mr Thomas acquired a vehicle to use as a "Travelling Shop" (the first in the area according to his advertisement in the Centenary issue of the Tiverton Gazette in 1958) which was driven by Clifford Buckingham. Later, the mobile shop was driven for a time by a Mrs Bucknell (whom Red taught to drive). The family soon outgrew the living accommodation at the shop and in about 1961 Glenys was able to buy Wharf House in Turnpike, which she ran as a Guest House while her husband ran the shop.

Mr Thomas took over the Post Office business on Mr Goffin's retirement in November 1951, moving it from Bridge House to Challis Stores; at that time, opening hours were 9.00am – 6.00pm six days a week Monday to Saturday, except Wednesday, which was 'half-day closing'. Although the Thomases rented the shop they lived at Wharf House, so the shop became vulnerable to break-ins, and there were minor thefts – mainly of cigarettes. Glenys remembered the worst incident, in 1962, when someone broke into the premises and emptied the Post Office safe. Soon afterwards the Post Office authorities removed their service from this shop to another shop in Higher Town.

During the early 1960s, Thomas' advertisements in the Sampford Peverell Parish News became more and more elaborate. Often a two page spread, they could include a poem, a sketch and an article. The underlying message was, invariably, that to shop at Challis Stores would save you time and money, once the cost of a return bus ticket to Tiverton was taken into account. Clearly, the competition from supermarkets there was their prime concern, rather than any competition with the Higher Town grocers. (See Appendix 2 for examples of his advertisements).

After the Post Office burglary, Red Thomas became very depressed and decided to sell the business, which he did late in 1964 or early in 1965. Red then worked as a roofer for a company which subsequently became

Challis Stores, now entirely in Challis Cottage, circa 1950s

3R Roofing Company. The shop was taken over by Robert (Bob) Salter, and he re-branded it as 'Salter's Stores'. There was already another branch of Salter's Stores Ltd in Willand, so for Robert Salter to take on the Sampford Peverell shop was an expansion of his business. A resident of the village, Jenny Holley, recalls that the shop was run by Stan and Betty Spridell at about this time, so perhaps they managed it, whilst Bob Salter concentrated on the Willand store. Salter's advertisements in the Parish News magazine were along more traditional lines than Thomas', proclaiming that he had 'the best goods at the lowest prices' and that bacon and cheese were his specialities. The shop was run under the name of Salter's Stores until 1971, during which time trading in groceries as an independent store became more and more difficult on account of increasing competition from supermarkets.

THE STORE WITH A RECORD

1830 CHALLIS STORES commenced business as a General Store, serving your Great-grandparents with horse-drawn vehicles.

1920 CHALLIS STORES continues business with progressive methods, being the first to mechanise with Model T Fords to serve your Grandparents.

1955 CHALLIS STORES continues expanding with progressive methods. First, as always, to develop Travelling Shops—to bring the Store to your door.

1958 CHALLIS STORES offers for the OLDEST INVOICE, produced before the end of May, THREE POUNDS WORTH OF GROCERIES, chosen by the winner in the Modern CHALLIS STORES.

With the compliments of
YOUR COUNTRY GROCER

E. L. THOMAS
THE COUNTRY GROCER
SAMPFORD PEVERELL
— Tel. 314 —

Tiverton Gazette centenary issue, 1958

January 1972 saw a change of ownership and management together with a change of name for the shop. It was bought from owner Charles Spring by Alan Young, who changed the name of the premises to 'Sampford Stores and Off Licence'. Alan Young's first change was to the product range on offer, which now included: 'Provi-

SALTER'S STORES LTD.
Grocers and Provision Merchants
SAMPFORD PEVERELL
Telephone 533

THE BEST GOODS
AT THE LOWEST PRICES

Bacon and Cheese
OUR SPECIALITIES

Also at WILLAND (Telephone: Sampford Peverell 492)

Parish magazine advertisement, February 1965

97

sions, Wines and Spirits, Bottled and Canned Beers, Draught Sherry', and local deliveries were offered. One year later a further significant change was made when the premises became the 'New V.G.

SAMPFORD STORES
And OFF LICENCE

THE NEW V.G. SELF SERVICE STORE

FRUIT & VEGETABLES   GROCERIES   COOKED MEATS & BACON

We offer easy shopping in a cheerful, bright and friendly atmosphere

We have a comparable range of reasonably priced goods with many special offers twice monthly

JENNIFER and ALAN YOUNG
Sampford Peverell 820533

Parish magazine advertisement, January 1973

Self-Service Store', offering fruit and vegetables, groceries, cooked meat and bacon, whilst still retaining its off-licence. The advertisements now boasted of 'special offers twice monthly', and the shop was run by Jennifer and Alan Young. 'VG' was a group of convenience stores, which was subsequently split up and re-branded either as 'Spar' or 'Alldays'. After 4 years of the Youngs running it, the shop was sold on in 1976 to Bob Cherry and his wife Margaret, who continued to operate the business in the same manner as their predecessors. However, the Cherrys' tenure did not last long either, and when Dave and Joyce Wright (who were in Sampford Peverell – from Exmouth – one day in 1977 to look at a building plot) saw the property for sale 'as a going concern', they decided to buy it. Following some alteration and refurbishment, their first day of trading was on August Bank Holiday Monday, 1977.

The business changed from being a member of the VG group to a member of a similar group of convenience stores, the APT Group; 'Special Offers' were advertised nationally and APT shops were expected to carry stock. Joyce particularly remembered a rep trying to get her to stock instant custard ("just add boiling water") but she protested that this was a rural area and milk was readily available so no one would buy the instant sort. Two weeks later, after adverts on TV, she had to eat her words and ask for a supply, as customers had been asking for the product. Indeed, the advertisement in the Parish magazine from January 1979 reflect a broadening of the range of products on offer to include 'oven baked bread, local clotted cream, confectionery, chemist's sundries, hardware, cards and stationery'.

Despite their best endeavours, it became clear by 1979 that the enterprise was not

Sampford Stores
and OFF LICENCE
GENERAL SELF-SERVICE STORE
Groceries, Provisions, Meat, Fruit and Vegetables, and Hardware

FREE DELIVERY   *SPECIAL FORTNIGHTLY OFFERS*

Dave and Joyce Wright   Telephone 820533
(Member of the Association of Private Traders)

Parish magazine advertisement, January 1979

making money and their accountant, Norman Snell, suggested that they could make just as much by letting out the ground floor for office space as they could by trading as a shop. As he himself was looking for office accommodation in the village, the Wrights closed the shop and Mr Snell rented the space for his Accountancy business – the upper floor domestic accommodation being let to the Wrights' son and daughter-in-law, Steve and Sally (née Trevelyan).

In about 1982 Mr and Mrs Wright junior moved out, to their own house in the village, and Mr Snell ended his tenancy of the office space. Mr and Mrs Wright senior sold the whole premises to a Mr Mann, who ran it as a

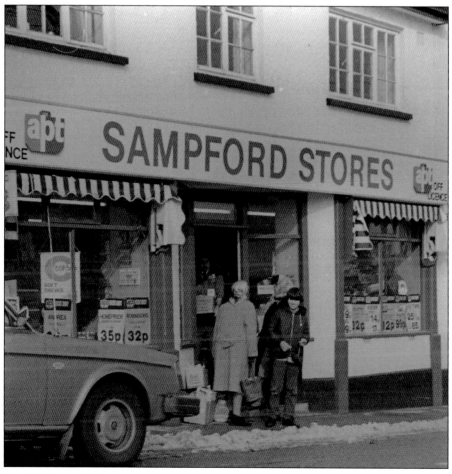

Sampford Stores, 1978

Photo: Ken Bass

hardware shop for about a year, at which point (about 1985) the commercial life of Challis Cottage finally came to an end. Despite its closure as a shop, the shop-front of Challis Cottage remained until 2001, when the building was completely refurbished to become the attractive cottage we can see today.

The former Handy Shop, circa 2000

Chapter 5

Newsagents

Introduction

In this age of round the clock television news and instant access to any website around the world via the internet, it is hard to imagine how scarce sources of news were in earlier centuries. Before the 19th century it would have been difficult for people in Sampford Peverell to find out what was happening in other parts of Devon, let alone the rest of the world. News arrived by word of mouth from people visiting or passing through, by the exchange of news in pubs, fairs and markets, or in some cases by correspondence with friends and relations. In the late 18th and early 19th centuries a few local and national newspapers began to appear. One such paper was Trewman's Exeter Flying Post which included occasional articles about Sampford Peverell, for example the 1777 story included in the chapter on Early Shops. A few national papers appeared in the early 19th century, but the numbers were limited as newspapers were taxed. Taxation on newspapers was removed in 1855, and this led to a rapid proliferation in the numbers of national and especially regional newspapers. In this part of Devon the weekly 'Tiverton Gazette and East Devon Herald' was founded in 1858, and the Western Times, which had grown out of the Exeter Weekly Times as a radical alternative to the conservative Exeter Flying Post, went daily in 1866. With levels of literacy increasing, the demand for printed news rose rapidly, and by 1890 newspapers and magazines could be found in even the remotest farmhouse or cottage.

The first reference to the sale of newspapers in Sampford Peverell occurs in the Western Times on 15th May 1866, which reports, under the heading 'Sampford Peverell', that "The agent for The Tiverton Times in this district is Mr J Darch who will receive orders for papers and advertisements."[32] There were two shoemakers in the village named John Darch, so he was probably one of these two.

The next reference is in Kelly's 1902 trade directory in which Joseph Jennings, who ran the Post Office, is described as a "news agent". This was when the Post Office was in Bridge House, Lower Town, near the canal bridge. After Mr Jennings' retirement that year his wife continued the Post Office business, which relocated to London House, Higher Town, from 1913 onwards, and Mrs Jennings was also described in the trade directories as a "news agent and stationer" until 1914, shortly before she also retired.

27 Lower Town - Barum House, 1914 - 1933

It is likely that the sale of newspapers moved at that time, as in his memoirs[35] Denis Cluett reported that during the First World War the newspaper business was run from Charles Jennings' shop in Lower Town, which was also referred to as 'the paper shop'. Charles Jennings was an interesting character and there is more about him in the chapter on Grocers and Drapers. Denis Cluett was a boy then, and later wrote:

> I think the thing which most endeared Charles to the village was his quite unselfconscious habit of riding his bicycle backwards. When he was delivering papers he thought nothing of riding around the village by sitting on the handlebars and pedalling along backwards. He seemed to have developed some sixth sense which enabled him to see exactly where he was going. We often used to watch him as he rode along the canal towpath in this manner, and we held our breath in the hopeful anticipation that he would end up in the canal, but he never did, much to our disappointment.

Denis Cluett also remembered that during the war:

Charles Jennings, riding his bicycle backwards

Illustration by Maggie Muggleton

only the morning papers were delivered at Sampford but an evening paper, 'The Express and Echo', was published at Exeter and distributed in Tiverton. If any particularly sensational news broke during the day the Express and Echo would rush out a special edition and a newsboy on a bicycle would be sent out from Tiverton with copies for sale. I still have vivid memories of one such special edition when the newsboy went through the village shouting 'Express and Echo Special! Special! Lusitania torpedoed, great loss of life! Express and Echo, Special! Special!' At the sound of the newsboy's shouts the village suddenly came to life and people dashed from all directions to buy the paper.

This would have been in May 1915.

Gregory's 1920 trade directory lists Albert Cornish, who lived in Higher Town, as a newsagent and shoemaker. Albert Cornish had previously worked at the Post Office and was later described as a shoemaker, so if he did have his own newspaper business he did not run it for long, but he may have been working for Charles Jennings who was still running the shop in Lower Town.

11 Higher Town - Rose Cottage, 1933 – late 1950s

Charles Jennings sold Barum House to Emily and Bill Upham in 1933, and the newspaper business moved to Higher Town soon afterwards. From 1935 onwards the trade directories list Herbert Thomas Morrell as a newsagent. Herbert Morrell, known as Bert, was born in Sampford Peverell on 8th May 1892 and spent most of his life in the village. In 1927 he married Iolen Hawkins, known as Ida, but they are not known to have had any children. They owned and lived in Rose Cottage, Higher Town, from which Bert ran their newspaper business for about twenty years. Local residents have shown us invoices from their shop spanning the whole period.

11 Higher Town (Rose Cottage) in 2018   *Photo: Peter Bowers*

Morrell's billhead, 1938
Courtesy of Ron Venner

We know more about Bert Morrell from former local resident Joan Howe, née Kingdom, whose parents ran the shop across the road from the Morrells. Bert Morrell had lost his sight, and Joan, who was still at school, used to help him. The papers were delivered to Sampford Peverell by train so Joan would go out to Sampford Peverell Halt, the site of the current Tiverton Parkway station, with Bert. The people at the Halt sorted his newspapers into order and Joan accompanied him on his delivery round, going out to Waterloo Cross and then back to Sampford Peverell where she left him to carry on alone. Despite his blindness Bert Morrell rode a bicycle, and cars parked outside the Kingdoms' shop often suffered bumps and scratches as he collided with them. Joan also took care of the billing for newspapers and was paid 6d a week. Bert had a large wireless set that was specially adapted for use by the blind and Joan remembers being with Bert when Prime Minister Neville Chamberlain made his announcement in 1939 that Britain was at war with Germany.

Another village girl, Pat Upham, whose parents ran the Barum House shop, also told us that Bert Morrell received daily and weekly papers at his house in Higher Town next to Mrs Snell's shop (Halls, 11a Higher Town) and delivered them on his bike. Although blind, he managed to deliver the papers accurately to the right houses. Some said he rode his bike with the papers but Pat only saw him pushing the bike, using it to carry their considerable weight.

27 Lower Town - Barum House, late 1950s - 1999

Bert Morrell died on 25th April 1959, but by then he had given up the newspaper business which was taken over by the Uphams at Barum House. An advertisement in the Parish Magazine in April 1958 placed by the Uphams includes the fact that they provided "Daily deliveries of Newspapers and Periodicals." Former local resident Martin Reid recalls that he "did a newspaper delivery round from this shop in the 1950s,

LET

W. UPHAM

SUPPLY YOU AS HE HAS DONE FOR 27 YEARS
with Groceries, Fruit and Vegetables, Confectionery, Cakes and Sliced
Bread, Aladdin Paraffin. Daily deliveries of Newspapers and Periodicals.
Orders Delivered near and far — Agents for " The Welfare Foods "
Phone : SAMPFORD PEVERELL 286

Tiverton Gazette, 29 April 1958

and found Bill Upham and his wife a very pleasant couple, in spite of his reputation for being strict, which was probably due to his other role as a Special Constable."

The Uphams sold the shop in 1966 to Ken Knowles, who continued the newspaper business and employed five boys to deliver the papers. We have been told that the most efficient of these boys was a lad who could barely read, but he always knew, before he left the shop, if Ken Knowles had made a mistake in the numbering. The other boys did not usually spot mistakes until they were out delivering the papers, so they had to sort them out en route, which took time and often made them late for school. Ken Knowles was responsible for the deliveries of newspapers in Uplowman, Whitnage and the surrounding district as well as Sampford Peverell.

The newspaper business stayed in Barum House for a good many years. When Mike and Mavis Gee took over the shop in 1977 it only sold newspapers and a few odds and ends so they expanded the range of the goods they sold. A parish magazine advertisement in 1985, when Barum House was being run by Robert and Gill Sweetman, still described it as "your local village stores, newsagent and off-licence". The Sweetmans were followed in 1986 by Jill and Chris Gabbey, who continued to provide local newspaper deliveries until they eventually closed the shop in 1999.

21 Higher Town - London House, 1999 - 2010

Philippa Flatters remembers that when she, with her husband Peter and their family, arrived in the village in 1999 to run the Post Office in London House, newspapers were being sold from Kelland's garage in Lower Town, but when the garage closed down soon afterwards the villagers asked them to take on the newspaper business at the Post Office. The newspapers were delivered to the shop by van from Exeter. The Flatters' had to get up very early to sort them out, and even then people would be queueing outside waiting for the shop to open. The Post Office changed hands again in 2008, but papers and magazines were still sold there until it closed in early 2010.

Smithys Way - SPAR shop, 2010 - today

Since the London House Post Office closed in 2010 the newspaper business has been run from the Spar shop in Lower Town where people still like to buy the news in printed form – but for how much longer?

Chapter 6

The Post Office

Introduction

The General Post Office was established in this country in 1660, but it was very different from the postal service we know today. A network of Post Offices was set up where senders could take items for delivery. These items were sent to sorting centres, and then on to the receiver, who could choose whether to accept the item (and pay for it) or not. Mail was transported by horse-drawn coach. Payment rates varied with distance, size and location, and there were a lot of inconsistencies and problems with the system.

Many improvements were introduced in the 19th century. From 1838 onwards mail could be transported by train which improved the speed of delivery, and in 1840 Rowland Hill introduced a prepaid service using stamps which could be bought at a low and universal charge of one penny. This charge remained in place until 1918 when it was increased to a penny halfpenny.

1853 letter with Sampford Peverell postmark

Pillar boxes came into use in the 1850s; before this, senders would have to take letters to a receiving house (effectively an early Post Office) or wait for the Bellman who wore a uniform and walked the streets collecting letters from the public, ringing a bell to attract attention. The Post Office Savings Bank was set up in 1861. In 1870 postcards were introduced, and the Post Office was given control of the telegraph service so telegraph facilities became available around the country. Postal Orders[33] became available in 1881, and parcel post in 1883. The introduction of the state 'old age pension' in 1909, which had to be collected from a local Post Office, also turned Post Offices into weekly meeting places. All these changes greatly increased the use and importance of the village Post Office.

The first mention of a postal worker in Sampford Peverell is in the 1841 census which records that John Strong, a man in his 20s who lived in Lower Town, was a postman. The Post Office is first referred to in a Western Times advertisement of 23rd December 1843. Personal advertisements usually gave a Post Office code and address as the place for replies, like the PO Box numbers which are still used today. This advertisement says "To Servants. Wanted, a steady, active youth, accustomed to the care of a horse, and to make himself useful both in the house and garden. He must have a good character from his last place, and not be under sixteen. Address, A.Z., pre-paid, Post Office, Sampford Peverell, near Tiverton."

10 Lower Town – 1851 – 1881

The next reference we have to the Post Office is in White's Directory of 1850, which lists businesses including "Post-Office at W.Taylor's. Letters via Tiverton". This refers to William Taylor, a tailor then 69 years old, who lived in Lower Town, and about whom there is more in the chapter on Tailors. In the 1856 Kelly's Directory he is listed as both "tailor and postmaster" and in the 1857 Billing's Directory it says "Post Office – Mr. W. Taylor, Sub-Postmaster. Delivery, 9.30 a.m.; despatch, 4.30 p.m. Nearest Money Order Office, Tiverton." By the end of the year people did not have to go so far to find a money order office because the Exeter Flying Post of 5th November 1857 announced that "Money order offices are to be opened at the Post Offices of Modbury, Sampford Peverell, Witheridge, and Woodbury, in this County." Money orders were paper certificates for specific sums of money which could be sent to someone, rather like cheques. The Post Office took over the system in 1838 but in 1881 it was replaced by the Postal Order system[33].

By 1861[17] William Taylor, still working at the age of 78, was described as "tailor and sub postmaster' living in "Post Office", which is listed next to the Globe Inn so it was almost certainly in one of the Challis properties, probably Challis House, which at that time seemed to be split into two shops. There are still traces of a letter box inside Challis House. William Taylor died later that same year, in December 1861, and soon afterwards the Post Office business was taken over by Joseph Jennings.

Joseph Jennings was born in Sampford Peverell in 1831, the son of John Jennings, a plumber and glazier, and his wife Elizabeth née Hewett. Prior to becoming postmaster Joseph was a grocer and shopkeeper who in 1861, aged 29, was living in Higher Town with his 47-year-old wife, Martha. Also living with them were Martha's father John Parr, and her niece Rosa Martha

Parr, then 6 years old. Joseph's older brother Richard was a plumber and glazier living in Halls, Higher Town, and his younger brother William ran a shop in Lower Town, about which there is more in the chapter on Grocers and Drapers.

Challis House in 2018   Photo: Peter Bowers

Joseph Jennings was clearly a busy man: in Kelly's Directory of 1866, as well as being "grocer & draper, coal & salt dealer" he is listed as the postmaster at the "Post & Money Order Office & Post Office Savings Bank ... Money orders are paid & granted from 9 to 6". We can't be totally sure of the location of the Post Office – it may have been in his old shop in Higher Town, but he probably moved to where William Taylor had had the shop in Lower Town, near the Globe. The Post Office was definitely there by 1870 when the Land Tax Return lists him as the occupier of 'Challis', now known as Challis House. The 1871 census shows Joseph and Martha Jennings in the Post Office in Lower Town, with Martha's niece, Rosa, now working as an assistant there.

In 1870 Joseph Jennings wrote to the local newspaper to correct a statement suggesting that the Savings Bank was new: "a Money Order and Savings' Bank business has been conducted at this office for many years, and on Wednesday, the telegraph was also established at this office". By 1873[34] it was described as a "Post & Money Order & Telegraph Office & Post Office Savings Bank". Letters arrived from Tiverton at 8.00 am and were dispatched at 5.40 pm. Mr Jennings was still also working as a grocer, draper and coal dealer. The Jennings were in Challis House until around 1873, when, the shop was taken over by Mr F Taudevin. This ties in with a 1913 newspaper obituary which stated that in his early life "Mr Jennings kept a general shop in the village. About forty years ago he disposed of this to the late Mr F W Taudevin, and devoted himself to his duties of sub-postmaster and newsagent." There is more about Taudevin's shop in the Chapter on Grocers and Drapers.

Joseph Jennings moved to premises opposite the East Devon County School in Lower Town. His new Post Office was probably in part of Kings Cottages, now the site of a pair of semi-detached houses next to Coronation Cottages. In November 1875 a newspaper reported a case, believed to be arson, when 'an alarming fire' in an adjoining barn destroyed the Post Office: "Mr Jennings was ill in bed and had to be helped out of his smoke-filled room. The school's headmaster helped him over to the school. The barn and another old building attached to it were almost totally destroyed. The roof of the Post Office was destroyed and the interior gutted. None of the furniture or materials belonging to the postal department were burnt, but some of the former was much damaged whilst being taken from the house." "Telegraphic communication was of course stopped, but the Head Postmaster of the district paid a visit to the place on the following day and made temporary arrangements for carrying on the postal work."

2 Lower Town – Bridge House 1881 – 1913

At some point between the 1875 fire and the 1881 census Joseph Jennings, his wife Martha, and Rosa Parr (Martha's niece and Post Office assistant) started running the Post Office from the newly-built Bridge House, which was owned by Joseph, and is situated by the canal bridge in Lower Town. Kelly's directory for 1883 reported that letters arrived from Tiverton at 8.00 am and were dispatched at 5.45 pm. A few years later in 1889 Kelly's directory said that letters were arriving earlier and leaving later: "Letters arrive from Tiverton at 7.15 am: dispatched at 7 pm. Money orders are paid & granted from 8 am to 6 pm & postal orders from 8.00am-8.00pm." They clearly worked long hours and handled a lot of business. As well as running the Post Office, Joseph Jennings was a trustee of the Methodist Chapel, appointed in 1888, along with his brothers Richard and William. It is likely that they were related to the Samuel Jennings who played a leading role in getting the chapel built.

Martha Jennings died in 1896, but Joseph, now 64, and his step-niece Rosa, now 40, continued to run the Post Office in Bridge House. The relationship between Joseph and Rosa was to become more than a business one; they were married in London that same year. A photo of the Post Office in the late 1890s shows several uniformed postal workers, a smartly dressed gentleman and lady, a lady with a bike, and a couple of delivery boys. Joseph and Rosa may well be the couple in the centre of the photo.

Post Office at Bridge House 1890s

The 1901 census shows them in Bridge House with a lodger, Edward Moysey, 22, who worked as a letter carrier. The following year the trade directory shows more postal services being offered. As well as the functions mentioned before, it specifies Express Delivery, and Parcel Post. Letters now arrived from Tiverton twice a day and there were also two dispatches a day. The telegraph business was open from 8.00 am to 8.00 pm, and on Sundays from 8.00 am to 10.00 am.

In 1902 the Post Office was transferred from Joseph to Rosa. His later obituary says this was because he had reached the official age limit, which must have been 70. Mrs Rosa Martha Jennings was now the sub-postmistress, and also a newsagent and stationer. The 1906 directory stated that there was now "no Sunday delivery", and gave the times when the letter boxes at "Ayshford (Wall letter box), Witnage *(sic)* and Leonard Moor" were cleared, twice a day. The 1910 directory added that the "Mount Pleasant Letter Box" was also cleared twice a day. The 'Mount Pleasant' Edward VII letter box was later moved around the corner into Boobery, where it is still in use.

According to the 1911 census they were still living at the Post Office, now with another lodger, Sidney Manners, 17, born in London, who worked as

Thomas Parkhouse, postman circa 1910

a Postal and Telegraph Messenger. They were also helped by Tryphena Ponsford, 18, a post girl, and daughter of Thomas Ponsford, the tailor, and by Tom Parkhouse, who was also a shoemaker.

In the 1910 survey[2], in this case probably written up a few years later, after the business had moved, the "Post Office" at Bridge House is listed as owned by Josiah Richards and occupied by Rosa Jennings. It is described as a "Cob stone and plastered Cottage, formerly a shop. Small garden in front." The ground floor contained a sitting room, two kitchens and a washhouse, and the first floor had three bedrooms. It was in 'fair repair", with a market value of £120.

21 Higher Town - London House 1913 – 1917

Joseph Jennings died in 1913 at the age of 92. In June of that year a newspaper article reported that Bridge House had changed hands, so the Post Office business was moving to the building in Higher Town formerly known as London House or the London Inn. There is more about London House in the Chapter on Grocers and Drapers. According to Kelly's 1914 directory, letters now arrived from Tiverton three times daily and were also dispatched three times a day.

Rosa Jennings retired in 1915 when she reached the age of 60, and on 1st May 1915 Maud Taylor, an assistant in the Post Office for many years, was appointed sub-postmistress. Maud, born on 19th February 1876, was a granddaughter of the William Taylor who was postmaster in the 1850s. In 1891 she was still living with her parents and her brother, Arthur, in Higher Town, but in 1901, aged 25, she lived in Torquay and worked in the railway refreshment room, along with two other young women living in the same lodging house. By 1911, now 35, she was back in Higher Town, Sampford Peverell, nursing her consumptive older brother who died that same year. She may have been appointed sub-postmistress in 1915 due to the shortage of men in the village caused by the First World War. In his reminiscences[35] Denis Cluett wrote that Miss Taylor was "a rather sweet but very dreamy middle-aged spinster". He also said that telegrams were assumed to bring bad news so there was never any hurry about delivering them.

> If one arrived for someone in one of the outlying farms Miss Taylor would wait until the end of school and then get one of the children going in that particular direction to deliver it. Telegrams for anyone in the village proper were delivered by Bert Cornish, and what with his one good leg and two crutches he was not a notably fast mover. In addition to this he was in the habit of stopping to discuss the contents of the telegram with everyone he happened to meet. Although this made for rather long delivery times, thanks to the astonishing efficiency of the village bush telegraph it usually happened that the person to whom the telegram was addressed knew all about it before the actual message arrived.

In August 1916, the Parish Council minutes record that they decided to write to the postmaster at Tiverton about "the great inconvenience and loss occasioned to us and the inhabitants generally by the retarded deliveries of letters here introduced on August 14th. What we regard as essential is that the first and second deliveries should be as hitherto, which we understand is fully practicable if the connection with the mail train at Tiverton Junction be maintained." We don't know what reply, if any, they received to this letter. Perhaps it got lost in the post...

The following year the Post Office was in the news because in 1917 Maud Taylor was found guilty of fraud and of falsifying accounts. One witness, Charles Ponsford, who worked as her assistant for two years, said "it often happened when people came to cash vouchers they were unable to be paid as there was not sufficient money in the till. On these occasions defendant would send him out into the village to borrow money, and if we was unable to get it the customers were told it would be forwarded to them. He sometimes, at defendant's instructions, took money from the till to do 'shopping' for her." The prosecutor told the jury they would hear that "almost daily the defendant would send out two or three times for a noggin [a quarter of a pint], or a noggin and a half, of spirit, and when they remembered that this would cost about 5s or 6s [5 or 6 shillings] they would easily understand where the money had gone." This, of course, may explain the dreaminess that Denis Cluett remembered! In his memoir Denis Cluett said that she "had the misfortune to fall under the influence of a local man called Bert Cornish." He wrote that Bert helped out at the Post

Office as part-time postman and telegraph boy, and he seemed to enjoy complete freedom to use the Post Office and its contents as he wished. "When Miss Taylor was indicted the general opinion in the village was that Bert Cornish was the real culprit although no proof of this was ever found". During the court case Miss Taylor, when asked if she wanted to say anything, replied "I have been tempted from my commencement of postal duties to do all manner of things, that have not been right." She was sentenced to "12 months in the second division". Second division prisoners received slightly better treatment than 'ordinary' prisoners in that they were kept away from the others, received more letters and visits, and wore clothes of a different colour, so she was treated with some leniency. We can't be sure exactly what happened to her after her time in prison, but by 1939 she was living at the 'Home of the Good Shepherd, Holloway Street, Exeter', doing kitchen work but also there as an inmate[6]. The home was formerly a convent and refuge, but by 1939 it was a home for "mental defectives". The residents were all women, girls, and children, mostly described as "mentally defective" which covered a wide variety of problems at that time, and most did not have a job as they were "incapacitated". Maud, at least, was able to do some work there. She died in Exeter in 1952.

2 Lower Town – Bridge House 1917 - 1951

Soon after Maud Taylor's departure, on 6th December 1917, the Post Office business was taken over by Frederick Thomas Goffin, who was born in Sampford Peverell on 25th October 1877, the son of Frederick Thomas Goffin and his wife Elizabeth, née Farr. For many years he was a market gardener, living with his parents at Wharf House, Turnpike, where he still lived in 1911. A 1951 newspaper article about him says that he had formerly been a florist in Cullompton, but returned to Sampford due to ill health. When he took over he moved the Post Office back to Bridge House, the place it had occupied a few years earlier and which Mr. Goffin now owned. The article reports that "during his 34 years Mr Goffin has seen the postal services change and the duties of postmaster become more involved". In 1917, he paid out about 70 old age pensioners and allowances: today [1951] the number has increased to about 180".

In April 1937 the Parish Council decided to write to the Post Office Authorities asking them to "arrange for the erection of a telephone kiosk in the village." This resulted in a telephone box being set up near the canal bridge, close to the Post Office in Bridge House. The telephone and postal services must have been heavily used during the Second World War, when

Post Office at Bridge House, 1920s

friends and relations were away, and many US and English servicemen were lodged in the village. When Frederick Goffin retired in 1951 his long service in the Post Office was much appreciated and the Parish Council organized a retirement gift for him.

8 Lower Town – Challis Stores 1951 – c1963

Frederick Goffin and Edmund Thomas, 1951

Following Frederick Goffin's retirement the Post Office business moved down the road to Challis Stores, the proprietor of which, Mr E.L.H.Thomas, became the new sub-postmaster. Born in Cardiff, Edmund Levi Thomas, known as Red because of the colour of his hair, was in the RAF during the Second World War and spent five years as a prisoner of war. After his demobilization, he moved to Sampford Peverell in 1947 with his wife Glenys and baby son, Bruce.

In May 1952 the Parish Council wrote to the Postal Authorities asking "if the telephone line to the Kiosk near the Bridge could be disconnected from the phone at the Post Office. It often happened that after use of the Post Office the switch was left over and the telephone at the Kiosk was disconnected, causing delay and inconvenience to would be callers." They had to send reminders and eventually the line was separated from the Post Office number in February 1953. In 1955, at the Parish Council's request, a second telephone kiosk was installed in Boobery, near the new council houses in Beaufort Close. This red phone box was disconnected

Former phone box, now book swap, 2019
Photo: Heather Culpin

in 2018 and moved down to Lower Town where it serves as a book swap. The Council was told that the older phone box by the canal bridge would be moved - it was relocated to a position next to The Globe Inn. At some point soon after 1987 the old telephone kiosk by the Globe was replaced with a newer glass and metal model which was set up next to the village car park. This phone box was removed in 2018 and replaced by the de-commissioned red phone box from Boobery. Neither phone box had been used for some time due to the widespread use of mobile phones.

Going back to Challis Stores, a robbery was reported there in The Times newspaper on 25th April 1962: "Devon police are investigating a Bank Holiday theft from Sampford Peverell, near Tiverton, where a safe was forced open in a sub-post office and more than £1800 worth of stamps, postal and money orders, and £200 in cash were taken". Soon afterwards the Post Office authorities removed their service from the shop.

There had been a George V letter box in the wall of Challis Stores when the Thomases were there, but it was removed at around this time. There is also a George V letter box set into a brick column next to Coronation Cottages which is still in use. This may be the one which was inset into the wall of the cottages which once stood opposite Coronation Cottages - see far left of this photo.

On far left, wall post box opposite Coronation cottages, 1950s

21 Higher Town - London House c1963 – 2010

At some point between 1963 and May 1965 the Post Office business was moved back to 21 Higher Town, known as London House, the site it had occupied between 1913 and 1917 when it was run by Rosa Jennings and the unfortunate Maud Taylor. An advertisement in the Parish Magazine for May 1965 showed that it was being run by Rosalie and Walter Redstone.

Mrs Redstone had previously been Mrs Parkhouse and had helped her first husband run the shoe shop there. There is more about Parkhouse's shop

> Advertisement
>
> R. & W. REDSTONE
>
> Sampford Peverell Post Office, Higher Town.
>
> Stationery and Birthday Cards
>
> Pyrex
>
> Wellingtons, Slippers and Plimsolls

Parish magazine advertisement, May 1965

in the chapter on Shoes. Rosalie married Walter Redstone in 1963 and when she became postmistress soon afterwards they changed the name of the shop to Sampford Peverell Post Office. As well as postal services, the Redstones offered stationery and birthday cards, Pyrex ware, wellingtons, slippers and plimsolls.

An item in the Parish Magazine for August 1966 reported that Mrs Redstone was relinquishing her position as postmistress as she and her husband were retiring. The business was taken over by Mr Avery, known as Bert, and his wife. From January 1975 onwards they advertised that they were also selling shoes, birthday cards, batteries and toys. In September 1978

L. & A. AVERY

Post Office and Stores

HIGHER TOWN, SAMPFORD PEVERELL

Stockists for:—

Pirelli, Dunlop, Tuf, Avenue, etc.

Slippers, Wellingtons and Shoes

Birthday Cards   **Batteries**

TOYS

Parish magazine advertisement, January 1975

a notice in the Parish Magazine reported that "everybody in Sampford is extremely sorry to hear that Mr and Mrs Avery are retiring and going to live, for the present, in Tiverton. They have run our Post Office for about twelve years and have been most kind and courteous and unendingly patient with us all".

The Post Office was taken over by Colin and Heulwen Ferguson, who put a piece in the Parish Magazine in November 1978 saying that they "sincerely appreciate their welcome to the village" and hoped to be of service. From January 1979 onwards they were advertising the sale of stationery, greetings cards, toys, confectionery, household goods, wellington boots and plimsolls. They also sold jigsaw puzzles.

A local resident, Jeff Parsons, remembers Colin Ferguson as "a late middle-aged gentleman with a sweet wife. I remember him for several reasons: his unsmiling, and often severe, manner; the hold-up that took place in daylight in his shop and caused him to install a properly covered-in security glass wall to protect him from the public; and his one saving grace of listening to the test matches on the radio in the shop." Like the Averys before them, they ran the Post Office for about twelve years.

THE

POST OFFICE

HIGHER TOWN

SAMPFORD PEVERELL

Telephone 820313

Colin and Heulwen Ferguson

are at your service

Stationery, Greetings Cards, Toys,

Confectionery, Household Goods,

Wellington Boots, Plimsolls.

Parish magazine advertisement, January 1979

The Parish Magazine of August 1990 reported that since 25th June the new postmaster was Mr Mike Leary, whose mother was running the shop. They hoped to offer more items for sale including gifts and Christmas stocking fillers. Jeff Parsons remembers that Mrs Leary was named Elsie, and he describes Mike Leary as a pleasant young man. Mike Leary eventually bought another Post Office in Exeter, and sold the Sampford Peverell business in 1999 to Peter and Philippa Flatters.

Philippa told us that they took on the Post Office because Peter had been made redundant from his job in Bristol, and they thought the Post Office would provide a secure income and a good environment for their children to grow up in. Peter viewed it on a sunny Spring afternoon and the village seemed idyllic. There is much more about the shop side of the business in the section on London House. The Post Office authorities introduced a computer system in the early 2000s, allegedly bringing the Post Office into the 21st century. Phillipa told us that Peter was not a natural IT person but he eventually managed to master it.

The Post Office in 2006   *Photo: Peter Bowers*

They were both grateful for the help given to them by Linda Turner. She had worked in the Post Office when Mike Leary was running it, and continued to work there later under the van Bussels. The Flatters' say that "her calm manner and impeccable book keeping made a telling contribution to the smooth running of the Post Office across three regimes." They also enjoyed the daily banter with the regular postmen who collected from the Post Office twice a day: Rob in the morning and Graham in the afternoon. They were always helpful and friendly. There was another postman who luckily only came occasionally but after once kicking the family dog, Wags, he was always greeted with suspicion and a growl!

There is a George V letter box in the wall of the Post Office, probably installed there from another site when the Post Office moved to London House in the 1960s. The letter box could be opened from the inside so Peter Flatters' had a key, which proved very useful when someone managed to drop their car keys into the box! The letter box is still there but is no longer in use.

Running the Post Office, the Flatters' came to know everyone in the village, and it was a real meeting place, especially on pension days when the pensioners congregated there. Some of the customers were great characters, such as a rather malodorous tramp who was obviously very well educated and was always interesting to talk to. Eventually they became disillusioned with the Post Office management structure and conditions, did not want to be so tied down, and wanted a new direction, so they decided to sell it on, but they stayed in Sampford Peverell.

In 2007 the Flatters' sold the business to Mike van Bussel and his wife Nicky. Unfortunately for them, the Spar shop in the newly-built Smithys Way opened in 2008 and trade at the Post Office declined. In an interview in the Exeter Express and Echo Mr van Bussel said that they had also been hit by a downturn in the economy, and despite taking measures like adding a small off-licence, changing the layout, and staying open 12 hours a day, the store became economically unviable. One cold morning in January 2010 visitors to the Post Office found a note on the door saying that it had closed – a surprise and shock to everyone in the village.

3a, The Mews, Smithys Way, SPAR shop 2010 onwards

Fortunately for the village the Post Office business re-opened later that year in the Spar shop in Smithys Way, which is where it still operates today (2020). There is more about the Spar shop in the chapter on Shops in 2020. It provides all the basic postal services, and has a daily collection, as do the three letter boxes in the village: in Lower Town, Boobery, and Higher Town. To compensate for the closing of the letter box in the wall of London House, a new Queen Elizabeth II letter box was set up at the junction of Higher Town and Blackdown View. Pensions are no longer paid from Post Offices so the weekly gathering of pensioners has ended, but the shop still acts as a focal point for the village.

Letter boxes in the village in 2018   *Photos: Heather Culpin*

Chapter 7

Shoes

Introduction

Until the 20th century most items of clothing, including shoes, were produced locally, and this was the case in Sampford Peverell which had its own boot and shoemakers, or cordwainers. The term 'cordwainer' originally referred to someone who worked with 'cordovan', from 'Cordoba', a city in Spain which was a source of fine leather. Later 'cordwainers' came to mean shoemakers in general, with shoe repairers being called cobblers, who could be itinerant, going from house to house or village to village to mend shoes. Another old term for a shoemaker or his apprentice was a 'snob'. In the late 18th century Cambridge students started to use the shoemaking term 'snob' for anyone who wasn't a student, but it gradually morphed into its present meaning. In the records for Sampford Peverell there are frequent references to cordwainers, shoemakers, or boot makers, but we haven't found any cobblers or snobs in the village!

Shoe making was usually carried out in the home, where family members could help; expertise and tools were passed down from generation to generation. New shoemakers were trained up through the apprentice system: a young man would work, and probably live, with a master shoemaker and his family for seven years to learn the trade. He would then be qualified to work as a journeyman until he was accepted by the shoemakers' guild as a master craftsman, when he could set up in business for himself. In the cities the cordwainers were highly regulated, and associations of cordwainers were set up from the 1400s onwards; the Guild of Cordwainers in Exeter was set up in 1481. All shoemakers had to be literate to cope with regulations, prices and measurements, so their names often appear on legal documents as witnesses.

Shoes were sometimes made out of wood, or wood combined with leather, but in this area it is likely that they were made solely of leather, of which there was an ample supply as there were tanneries in and around Sampford Peverell. From the 16th century onwards welted shoe construction was the norm. This involved the upper part being sewn to a welt, or leather rim, with another row of stitches from the welt to the outer sole. This method of production and the tools used for it remained pretty much unchanged until the introduction of machinery in the 19th century. Shoes were traditionally not sewn with a needle - instead holes were created using awls through which a waxed linen thread was inserted with a pig's bristle.

Heels were added to footwear from the 1590s onwards. Lasts were needed to get the correct slope of the sole to fit the lift of the heel and as it was too expensive to keep a stock of lasts for different heel heights as well as for each foot, most footwear was the same for both left and right feet. This practice of making shoes with straight soles would continue for the next two hundred years, gradually falling from favour in the 19th century and only finally disappearing in the 1880s.

Once standardized shoe measurements were accepted by the shoemakers' guilds in about 1700, and making straight soles became easier, it became profitable for shoemakers to pre-make quantities of footwear. Footwear became the first ready-to-wear clothing article, sold through shoemakers' shops, haberdashers and "cheap shoe" warehouses, another name for off-the-peg retailers. Standardized measurements ensured a good fit for length, but width sizes were not introduced until 1880.

Shortages of leather footwear, especially for military use, caused problems in the late 18th and early 19th centuries. Shoes from those who had died were passed on, boots from those killed in battle were reused, and everyone looked for ways to shortcut the long years of apprenticeship needed to make a good shoemaker. Improvements included the use of pantographs to make mirror images of lasts, a sole-riveting machine for military footwear, and a press for cutting out leather. In 1823, the metal eyelet was introduced,

A shoemaker's apprentice, 1853

which eventually replaced the time-consuming task of hand stitching lace holes. With the perfection of the lock-stitch sewing machine by 1860, shoes could be made as quickly as the machine-sewn uppers could be attached to the soles.

The invention of the sewing machine was primarily initiated by the need for sewing leather, not cloth, more proficiently. Chain-stitching machines were introduced in early French shoemaking factories in the 1830s, but it was found to be more suitable for decorative work than seam construction. It was the American Isaac Singer's patented lock-stitch sewing machine for leather in 1856 that was to begin a series of major changes to the shoemaking industry over the next thirty years including a closing machine, a welting machine and a lasting machine. These machines made it possible to mass-produce footwear, as shoes could now be made at great speed and little cost. This was done at the Clarks' factory in Street, Somerset, the first shoe factory in the country. Mass production led to a gradual decline in hand shoemaking, as exemplified in Sampford Peverell where the number of shoemakers went down from 13 in 1841 to just three by 1921, and those three would have been mostly doing repairs rather than making shoes.

17th century Sampford Peverell shoemakers

The earliest reference we have found to a shoemaker in Sampford Peverell occurs in a 1609 property lease, to which "Christopher Blackaller of Sampford Peverell aforesayde, cordwayner" was a witness. The only other thing we know about him was that his will went through probate in Exeter in 1629, but the details have been lost.

A few years later, in 1620, a court case was brought by Alice Saunders against a person accused of stealing from her inn or "tippling-house". Alice is described in court as the "wife of John Saunders of Sampford Peverell in the said county, shoemaker".

Finally, in 1671 the will of Alexander Bower of Sampford Peverell went through probate in Exeter, and in this will he was described as a 'cordwinder', a variation of the word cordwainer.

18th century Sampford Peverell shoemakers

18th century apprenticeship records give us the names of three shoemakers and their apprentices. In 1759 Lewis Melhuish, a cordwainer, took on Thomas Curwood as an apprentice. Lewis died in 1766, but his son William continued in the business and took on Henry Brice as an apprentice in 1784. The third apprentice in the list was William Clark, who was taken on as an apprentice in 1783 by John Darch, a cordwainer.

Another 18th century cordwainer was Robert Webber. The Somerset Heritage Centre has details of a "lease by William Ayshford Sanford of Nynehead, Esq. to Robert Webber of Sampford Peverell, Devon, cordwainer, of a tenement at Bowbeere in the borough and parish of Sampford Peverell, Devon, 16 Jan 1796". This property was in Boobery, shown on the 1796 map as being roughly where number 12 is now. Robert Webber was probably the one baptised in Sampford Peverell in 1742, the son of John Webber. Another shoemaker in the village listed in the 1841 census, William Webber, was born in 1755, and was also the son of John Webber, so these two shoe-making Webbers were probably brothers.

The Darch family

The Darch family of Sampford Peverell was involved in the shoemaking business for at least 150 years from the mid 18th century (and perhaps earlier) until the late 19th century.

We have seen that John Darch took on an apprentice in 1783. He was probably the John Darch who was born in Sampford in 1727, but there was another shoemaking Darch in business at the same time. The 1841 census tells us that William Darch, then 80 years old, was a shoemaker. He was born in the village around 1761 and was probably John Darch's nephew. He was making shoes from the 1780s onwards, and well into the next century. He married Hannah Wilcox in 1785 and they had several children including Richard. Richard Darch was born in Sampford Peverell in 1802, and he married Miriam Hurford in 1836. They had a son, William, in 1837, but Miriam died two years later. Richard Darch didn't remarry, and brought up his son with the help of his unmarried older sister, Sarah Darch.

In 1815, when Charlotte Darch was baptised, the occupation of her father, Thomas Darch, was given as cordwainer. Thomas Darch was the youngest brother of the William Darch mentioned above, and uncle to Richard. He was born in Back Street (a lane joining Boobery to Higher Town) in 1774, and married Sarah Land in 1794. From 1796 to 1817 they had twelve children baptised in the parish church, at least two of whom became shoemakers: Thomas Darch, born in 1801, who married Mary Elworthy in 1824, and later changed his profession from shoemaker to gardener, and John Darch, born in 1806, who married Sarah Dunn in Sampford in 1830.

Another Darch shoemaker was mentioned in the parish records in 1838 when John Darch, cordwainer, and his wife Elizabeth, had a daughter called Arabella, the first of many children. This John Darch was born in Cheriton Fitzpaine in 1817, married a Sampford girl, Elizabeth Mutter, in 1837, and stayed in Sampford Peverell for the next 40 years or so. Henceforth we'll refer to him as John Darch CF (for Cheriton Fitzpaine). It seems likely that he was related to the other Darches, but we cannot be certain. According to the 1836-1840 Rate Book one of the John Darches lived in a cottage called 'Old Barn', but we are not sure which John Darch this was, or the exact whereabouts of Old Barn.

Shoemaking in Sampford Peverell seemed to reach a peak in 1841 when the 13 shoemakers and apprentices listed in Sampford Peverell included the octogenarian William Darch, who lived in Higher Town, and six other Darches: William's sons John and Richard, William's younger brother Thomas, and Thomas's sons Thomas and John, plus John Darch CF. The elderly William Darch died in 1846.

By the time of the 1851 census numbers had gone down but there were still eight cordwainers, shoemakers, or boot and shoemakers, in Sampford Peverell. Four of them were Darches in Higher Town: Richard Darch, and John Darch, who were cousins and lived almost next door to each other, Richard's older brother John who was lodging with Richard Southwood, the baker, and John Darch CF.

The following year, in 1852, a petition against the transportation of two local boys (see Appendix 1) was signed by several people in the village, including Richard Darch, who called himself a "cordwinder", and John Darch, who called himself a "boot and shoe maker". They were cousins of Thomas Darch, the shoemaker turned gardener, whose wife, Mary Elworthy, was an aunt of one of the boys involved.

Richard Darch's signature on 1852 petition
Courtesy of findmypast.co.uk

John Darch's signature on 1852 petition
Courtesy of findmypast.co.uk

By 1861 some of the Darches had died and others had moved out of the village. John Darch CF and his large family were living in Cross Hill, Higher Town. Elsewhere in Higher Town were Richard Darch and his 23-year-old son, William, a farm labourer, and Richard's nephew John Darch and his wife. One of these Darches is presumably the gentleman referred to in a newspaper report from January 1863 about an incident which also throws an interesting light on the uses to which Victorian underwear could be put. Emma Parker, a 16-year-old girl from Sampford Peverell, was found guilty of stealing from the farmhouse in Halberton where she was a servant. Mrs. Greaves, wife of the farmer, was suspicious of her, and as the girl was about to leave the house one Sunday afternoon Mrs. Greaves demanded to know what she had in her pocket. The pocket was empty, but:

Mrs. Greaves, though far from a lady of fashion, knew it possible that what was not outside the crinoline might be within, therefore, proceeded Mrs. Greaves, "I would take up her crinoline," and under the crinoline the fatal discovery was made. The Magistrate's Clerk rather shrunk from the further task of questioning the witness respecting the stowage of the stolen goods – he was not at all up in the knowledge of female dress. However, bound to fulfil his duty, he said to Mrs. Greaves, "You should not let your servant wear crinoline." "I don't let 'em wear it indoors," replied Mrs. Greaves, "but the girls now-a-day will hardly live with me if I won't let 'em wear it. I make 'em take it off again as soon as they come in for I'm afraid of the fire" – (a laugh). "Well, I lifted up the crinoline, and there in the pocket of the top petticoat I found this bottle of milk, which she took and gave to me." The bottle was produced, it was somewhere about a six ounce medicine bottle, marked for the several doses the patient was to take. There was also produced a small paper of smoking tobacco, and some slices of beef, wrapped in another paper, weighing three-quarters of a pound. "The rest" Mrs. Greaves said, "I took out myself. She then begged me to forgive her. I

The usefulness of the crinoline for fraud by Honore Daumier, 1857 from www.artic.edu/collection

asked her what she was going to do with it? And she said she was going to carry it to Darch's." Mrs. Greaves asked her "What Darch?" Prisoner said, "The gentleman Darch." Clerk – Who is he? Mrs. Greaves – I believe the shoemaker. Clerk – He's a bit of a swell then I suppose? Mrs. Greaves – Yes, sir (a laugh).

In the Exeter Flying Post the report explains that the phrase 'the gentleman Darch' was "a distinction bestowed on the village shoemaker for his natty regard to a fashionable exterior." There were no Darches in Halberton at that time, so he must have been one of the Sampford shoemaking Darches. The girl was found guilty and was sentenced to one week in prison with hard labour.

Richard Darch and his nephew John both died in the 1860s. This may explain the entry in the 1871 census for "Two uninhabited shoemaking workshops" in Higher Town, probably at the lower (Cross Hill) end of it. By 1871 the only Darch still working in the village as a shoemaker was John Darch CF. Soon afterwards he moved to Sidmouth with his second wife, to run a lodging house, thus bringing to an end the long Darch shoemaking tradition in the village.

Other shoemakers

William Dunn

William Charles Dunn was born in Halberton in 1840 and it was there that on 24th December 1863 he married Eliza Robertson, born in Beer but living in Halberton, the daughter of a Police Constable. Although only 20 he was already describing himself as a 'cordwainer'. William Dunn had relatives in Sampford Peverell: his aunt Jane was married to Richard Harris who ran a shop in London House in the 1850s. By 1871 William and his wife were living in Lower Town, where he was a shoemaker, she was a lace maker, and they had three children: one born in Halberton and two in Burlescombe. The youngest was just 2 years old so they had only recently moved to Sampford Peverell. They went on to have eleven children altogether: five boys and six girls. In the 1880s their teenage son Walter died, and two of

Halls, with (possibly) 'Cocky' Dunn in centre, outside workshop 1908

the other boys left home: one moved to Eastbourne and another emigrated to Australia. The family were Methodists, and in 1888 William Dunn was named as one of the trustees for the Methodist Chapel. In the 1890s the Dunns lived in Higher Town, and by 1900 they were in 'Halls', Higher Town, by which time 'Cocky' Dunn, as William was known, was one of just three shoemakers left in Sampford Peverell.

In Denis Cluett's memoirs there are descriptions of 'Cocky' Dunn as he was during the First World War, working behind the window in the shop attached to 'Halls'. Denis thought he was happy to have people watching him work but he didn't say much.

> Actually he was seldom capable of talking because his mouth was usually full of small brass tacks which we knew as sprigs. Cocky would fill his mouth with these and push them out between his teeth one at a time while he hammered them into the sole at a tremendous rate. Once or twice I remember him sneezing when his mouth was full and a shower of sprigs flew into all corners of the shop.

Denis was enormously proud when he was allowed to have his own heavy boots, known as watertights, made by Cocky Dunn, instead of having to wear 'normal' boots. He noted that all the men, boys and girls wore boots; it was only the ladies who wore shoes.

The war years must have been particularly difficult for him as two of his sons, both previously shoemakers living in London, were on active service. Archie was in the navy, and Alfred, in the army, spent 15 months as a prisoner of war, including 4 months in hospital. However, they both survived and returned to London but William's wife, Eliza, died in 1919. William Dunn continued working and was still listed as a shoemaker, and as a trustee of the Methodist Chapel, until his death in 1923.

Shoemaker at work in his shop

Illustration by Maggie Muggleton

The Parkhouse family

The 1881 census included Thomas Parkhouse, 18, a bootmaker's apprentice. Tom (as he was baptised) was born in Sampford Peverell in 1862, the son of George and Elizabeth Parkhouse, and in 1881 he was living with his parents and siblings in a cottage in Boobery. In 1882 he was a witness in what the local papers referred to as "The Sampford Stabbing Case".

John Parker, a Sampford Peverell baker, was charged with stabbing William Rich, one of three young men from Tiverton who went to Sampford Fair on 24th April 1882. After the fair the Tiverton men went to the Swan Inn in Halberton (which now serves as the Village Hall). Soon afterwards four Tiverton girls accompanied by four Sampford men, including Tom Parkhouse, also went into the pub and a few remarks were exchanged between the girls and the three Tiverton men which were "jocular" according to the men but offensive according to the girls. They all left at about the same time and started walking towards Tiverton, but the two groups passed each other a couple of times and a fight broke out between the men during which Rich was stabbed. One of the girls saw Parker with a knife but another said that he did not pull it open until the Tiverton men had gone. Tom Parkhouse testified that after leaving the Swan they were overtaken by the Tiverton men and Rich, taking hold of one of the girls, said, "This is my — girl", and

Victor Parkhouse outside his shop 1930s

hit Tom Parkhouse's friend, George Ponsford, leading to the fight, which Parkhouse tried to break up. At the trial it was said that without positive proof that Parker deliberately used the knife it would be unsafe to convict him, and the jury returned a verdict of not guilty. John Parker later married a Somerset girl and moved to Acton in west London where he continued working as a baker.

Tom Parkhouse married Clara Ponsford from Sampford Peverell and continued working as a shoemaker in the village. Tom and Clara, a dressmaker, lived in Boobery and had several children in the 1890s, by which time Tom had finished his apprenticeship. They were still living in Boobery in 1901, and Tom was now one of the three shoemakers in the village. By 1911 the Parkhouse family had moved from Boobery to Higher Town, and around this time Tom was described in the trade directories as both bootmaker and postman – there is a photo of him in Chapter 6 about The Post Office. He had been joined in business by his son Albert, 20, who later moved to Seaton and continued in the boot and shoe business there.

In 1929 Tom Parkhouse's son Victor Eli, who was born in 1901, became the owner and occupier of London House, 21 Higher Town, which he converted into a shoe shop. Tom died in 1931, leaving Victor Parkhouse as the last remaining shoemaker and shoe repairer in the village.

In the 1939 register Victor Parkhouse was listed as a 'shopkeeper footwear and outfitting dealer: boot and shoe repairer', and lived in London House with his older sister Edith. During the Second World War his niece and nephew, Jean and Stanley Trevelyan, the children of Daisy and William, would sometimes stay with them. There were British and American servicemen billeted in Sampford Peverell during the war, and Stan remembers that some American servicemen were billeted upstairs with the Parkhouses, and some British servicemen lived in the huge cellar of the building, which had big rooms with bunk beds, and, because it was built on a slope, it had windows and its own side entrance.

Victor Parkhouse married Rosalie Louisa Ball in Uffculme in 1944. They were both then in their 40s and did not have any children. The shop stayed in business a long time but changed from making shoes to selling and repairing them. An advert in the parish magazine in the early 1950s describes them as an agent for "Dunlop, John White, Holdfast, Dryfoot, and many other leading makes. Also a prompt repair service".

Victor died in 1953 but his widow kept the shop running. An advertisement in the parish magazine of December 1957 under the name of Mrs. V E Parkhouse offers "Ladies and gents footwear, good wearing shoes for children, cricket and football boots, wellingtons and plimsoles [sic]. Repairs given prompt attention by Mr. S Trevelyan on the premises.' Mr. S Trevelyan was her nephew, Stan, who has told us he did not much enjoy this shoe repair work and was delighted when National Service took him away from it! By December 1961 the shop was also dealing with Dry Cleaning, Pyrex glassware, and Addis ware. It continued to advertise in this style until 1962. In 1963 Rosalie Parkhouse married Walter Redstone. Also around this time the Post Office business in Lower Town closed, and Mrs. Redstone became the new postmistress, setting up the Post Office in what was the shoe shop. They changed the name of the shop and an advertisement from May 1965 describes the business as "R & W Redstone, Sampford Peverell Post Office, Higher Town. Stationery and Birthday Cards, Pyrex, Wellingtons, slippers and plimsolls". So shoe sales had not entirely disappeared from the village.

Tiverton Gazette, 29 April 1958

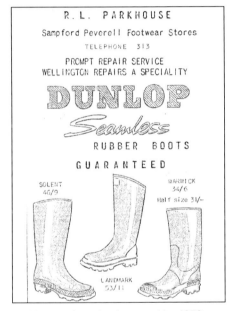

Parish magazine advertisement, May 1958

The Redstones retired in 1966 and the Post Office was taken over by Mr and Mrs Avery who continued to sell some footwear. In 1976 they advertised "Pirelli, Dunlop, Tuf, Avenue etc, slippers, wellingtons and shoes, birthday cards, batteries and toys". The Post Office under various owners continued to sell wellingtons and plimsolls well into the 1980s, but by the time Philippa and Peter Flatters were running the Post Office in the early 2000s the only items of footwear sold were flip-flops, and with the closing of the Post Office at that site in 2010 footwear sales in Sampford Peverell came to an end.

Other 19th and 20th century shoemakers and retailers

A shoemaker in the village in 1815 was William Gibbins, or Gibbons, described as a cordwainer when his daughter Elizabeth was baptised here. He had married Thomasin Hussey in 1814 somewhere in the Tiverton area, but the family did not appear again in the parish records.

In the 1830s several children were born to James Snow, cordwainer, and his wife Eliza. James Snow was born in Sampford Peverell in 1805 and worked in the village as a shoemaker until the 1850s. In 1841 the Snows lived at Moorend, Lower Town, and in 1851 they were still in Lower Town, but soon after this they moved to Bristol.

According to the 1841 census the 13 shoemakers and apprentices in Sampford Peverell included John Druller, 50, who lived with his wife, Elizabeth, in part of High Cross House. Elizabeth Druller died here in 1845, and he married again in Ottery St Mary in 1847, though still giving his occupation as cordwainer and his residence as Sampford Peverell. He died in the Tiverton area the following year.

Another shoemaker listed in 1841 was John Bailey, who married Eliza Needs, née Vickery, in 1847, but they moved to Bridgwater. It's likely that Eliza's first husband, James Needs, was related to other shoemaking Needs family members in the area.

William Webber, born in 1755, was still working as a shoemaker in 1841. Coincidentally, William Webber and William Darch, both octogenarians and living in Higher Town, died within days of each other, and were both buried in the parish churchyard in January 1846.

John Webber also lived to a good age. He was born in Exeter in 1781 and lived in Boobery. He never married. He was still described as a shoemaker in 1861, at the age of 81, but died later that year.

John Elworthy was first named as a Sampford shoemaker in 1841, when he was living in Lower Town and had an apprentice, Francis Needs. He was born in Exeter in 1791 and never married. In 1851 he was still in Lower Town, working as a boot and shoemaker, but living with the blacksmith James Vickery and his family. He probably died in the 1850s.

A new name in 1851 is Henry Harris, 52, shoemaker, who was born in Washfield and was lodging at the Hare and Hounds at the time of the census, so he was probably just a visitor.

Francis Needs, another signatory to the 1852 petition (see Appendix 1), may well have been related to the other Needs shoemakers included in

Francis Needs' signature on 1852 petition
Courtesy of findmypast.co.uk

this chapter. He was born on 12th April 1820 and was baptised a few weeks later as a non-conformist, the son of Francis and Elizabeth Needs of Sampford Peverell. He seems to have switched between two jobs. In the 1841 census he was an apprentice to shoemaker John Elworthy, in Lower Town, but in the 1851 census he was a malt worker working for the maltster, Henry Broom, in Lower Town. A year later he signed the 1852 petition as a "shoemaker", but by 1871 he had moved to Uffculme and was working there as a brewer's general servant in the George Inn, where he was still working, as an ostler, in 1881. He never married, and was back in Sampford Peverell, listed as a shoemaker, in Always Cottage in 1891. He died and was buried here in 1893.

Another local shoemaker in the 1850s and 1860s was William Podbury, who was named as a shoemaker in the 1850s trade directories, so he probably had his own business. William Podbury was from Kentisbeare, and he and his wife Elizabeth, from Broadhembury, had three children baptised in Sampford Peverell. In 1861 they were living in Chains Cottage, but by 1871 they had moved to Honiton and later still they moved to Burlescombe.

When Henry and Ann Wood had their son William Henry baptised, in October 1854, Henry was described in the parish register as a cordwainer; however by 1861 he was a harness maker and later a saddler, which became his main business, so he was using his leather-working skills for other purposes. There will be more about him in a future publication on other businesses in Sampford Peverell.

Towards the end of the 1860s a son was born to shoemaker John Needs, and his wife Mary. John Needs was born in Holcombe Rogus in 1831, and married Mary Stevens there in 1857. They went on to have several children and from the 1870s to the 1890s he and his family lived in Higher Town. Mary died in 1899, but in 1900 he married Elizabeth Rolestone, who is mentioned in our chapter on butchers. The 1903 trade directory tells us that he lived, and had his business, in Coombe Cottage, which no longer exists but was at 24, Higher Town. He died in 1905, aged 74.

A couple of other shoemakers are mentioned in the Sampford Peverell marriage registers in the 1860s, namely Henry Holcombe and William Commins, but they came here to marry local girls, Sarah Elizabeth Goffin and Sarah Saunders, and then went to live elsewhere in the county.

Kelly's trade directory for 1866 includes a new name: John Towell, boot and shoe maker. He was from Halberton, and in 1871 was back in Halberton, so was not resident in Sampford Peverell for long.

In the 1870s the local shoemakers included Mark Lovell who came from Halberton and who had been a shoemaker since he was 14. He was married to Hannah Robertson from Beer and two of their children were born in Sampford Peverell, but they must have moved to Bradninch around 1877.

It was common practice for publicans to have a second trade, and a Sampford Peverell resident who had a sideline in shoemaking was Edward

Leach, landlord of the Hare and Hounds in Lower Town (now Coronation Cottages). He was listed in the 1873 trade directory as being both landlord and a boot and shoemaker. He came from Cullompton and lived in the Hare and Hounds with his wife and mother from around 1860 until he moved to Halberton in the late 1870s.

The 1881 census included three teenaged shoe makers: Tom Parkhouse, 18, William Broom, 15, and John Blackmore, 14. William Broom was born in Halberton but had lived with his parents, Henry and Elizabeth, in Higher Town since he was five. He must have left the area in the 1880s. John Blackmore was born in Sampford Peverell and also lived in one of the Boobery cottages with his grandparents - his mother, Mary, had been a single mother. He died of TB in 1884, aged just 18.

There are two new names in 1891: Thomas and James Morgan, aged 25 and 27. In the 1897 Kelly's trade directory they are described as grocers, ironmongers, and boot warehousemen. They were the sons of Elizabeth Morgan, a widow born in Culmstock who was a grocer and draper with a shop in London House, Higher Town – there is more on her in the chapter on Grocers and Drapers. From the description of them as 'boot warehousemen' it appears that they were not shoemakers but were selling cheap boots and shoes from the grocers and drapers shop; ready-made footwear had arrived in Sampford Peverell, accelerating the decline in shoe making in the village.

By the early 1900s only three shoemakers were working in Sampford Peverell: John Needs in Coombe Cottage in Higher Town, William Dunn in Halls, Higher Town, and Tom Parkhouse in Boobery.

A new shoemaker is mentioned in the 1911 census in Lower Town - Harry Capron, born in Wellington in 1873. He had a wife and five children, most of whom were also born in Wellington but the youngest, aged 8 months, was baptised in Sampford Peverell in October 1909. He was not listed in the trade directories so probably worked for someone else, and does not appear to have stayed long in the village.

Finally we come to Albert Cornish, born in Hillfarrance, Somerset, to Eli and Elizabeth Cornish. By 1911 he was living with his family in Higher Town, and was a shoemaker's apprentice. He served in the army during the First World War, as did his older brother Thomas who died fighting in France in 1917. Another brother, William, served in the Navy. Albert returned to Sampford after the war and worked as a newsagent and shoemaker. He did not marry and died in February 1936, aged 44.

Chapter 8

Tailors

Introduction

The word 'tailor' goes back to the thirteenth century and derives from the French word 'tailleur', meaning a cutter, in this case a cutter of cloth. Associations and guilds of tailors began in medieval times to control the craft of garment making, enforce standards, and oversee the apprenticeship system. An apprentice would spend years learning his trade with a master tailor, before becoming a journeyman, and eventually a master tailor in his own right, if approved by the guild. Clothes were expensive and were kept for as long as possible; indeed in many wills we find people bequeathing their clothes to their relations, who would have altered and re-used them. When Ambrose Curwood of Sampford Peverell died in 1593 he left all his tannery equipment and stock to his brother, and he also left him "all my wearing apparel". Mary Billinghay, a gentlewoman of Sampford Peverell, died in 1594 and left "all my apparrell in the trunk in the gallery" to her sisters, and to other relatives she left two aprons and a ruff. It was only the very rich who could afford to get new clothes made to keep up with fashion; most people just bought or took over essential clothes, getting them altered as necessary and enhancing them with accessories. The skills of seamstresses and tailors were needed both for making new clothes and for altering used ones, and Sampford Peverell had its own tailors, some with shops and some working from home. As was the case with shoemakers, master tailors were usually literate, so their names often appear as signatories on documents such as wills and leases.

The arrival of mechanisation and mass production methods were slower to affect tailors than many other craft workers. Sewing machines were developed in the 19th century and were being mass produced and made widely available by thc 1870s, but women's and children's clothes were more likely to be made at home than men's wear. Consequently the number of tailors did not decline as rapidly as the number of seamstresses until cheap ready-to-wear clothing became widely available in the 20th century. Even then there were still bespoke tailors in most towns for those who wanted their shirts or suits to be made to measure.

17ᵗʰ and 18ᵗʰ century tailors

The first Sampford Peverell tailor whose name we know was John Poole. On 10ᵗʰ January 1607 he signed a receipt to confirm that he had received goods previously belonging to a Walter Burman, and took full responsibility for them. The receipt begins "all men shall know by these present[ment]s that I, John Poole of Sampford Peverell in the county of Devon, Tailor, have received of John Trevelian of Nettlecombe in the county of Somerset, Esquire, all the goods and chattels of Walter Burman, deceased late servant unto the said John Trevilian".

The next tailor we know of in Sampford, from a list of wills, was Humphrey Drake, who was baptised in 1690, the son of a John Drake. He had a house in Boobery, one of the cottages referred to as 'Drakes and Rows', where 8 and 10 Boobery are now situated[8]. He died and was buried in Sampford in 1743.

In a lease for Cross Hill dated 12ᵗʰ February 1700, Humphrey Marsh leased the property to his son-in-law John Jutson (sometimes spelt Jutsum). Humphrey Marsh wrote that this was "in consideration of his Naturall love & affection which he hath and bears that unto Hannah his Daugher now the wife of John Jutson of Sampford Peverell aforesaid Taylor & her children". It also explains that the Jutsons were already occupants of Cross Hill, so this

Houses formerly known as 'Drakes and Rows', Boobery, in 2018   Photo: Peter Bowers

Cross Hill in 2019   Photo: Peter Bowers

is almost certainly where John Jutsum conducted his tailoring business. Hannah and John had twelve children christened between 1695 and 1714. John Jutsum died in 1725 and his widow Hannah died in 1732.

Next we have Benjamin Croydon, who was baptised in Willand in 1697. In 1747 he took on John Bale from Halberton as a tailor's apprentice, and in 1753 he stood as guarantor for three licensed victuallers (innkeepers) in the village, giving his occupation as maltster, so he combined the two occupations. Benjamin Croydon's name regularly appears in the Land Tax returns as one of the two collectors of Land Tax in the village between 1752 and 1759 so he must have had some standing in the community. He himself was the occupier of a property called Fullers, which we think was on the north side of Turnpike in the area of numbers 5 to 7, from 1755 to 1772, but by 1774 it was described as "late Croydon's" so he must have moved on. He was buried in Sampford Peverell in 1782.

Interestingly two of the other licensed victuallers in 1753 were backed by John Drake (probably related to the Humphrey Drake mentioned earlier), who was also a tailor. Three John Drakes were baptised in the village between 1711 and 1718 so he was probably one of those. John Drake paid tax on a property called Mitchell's from 1744 to 1753, but we are not sure exactly where it was. He died in 1772.

Another tailor involved in the alcohol business was Roger Hellier. In his role as a tailor he took on six apprentices between 1759 and 1793: Robert Prickman, James Grant, David Spark, John Webber, Robert Mutter, and William Bidgood. In the licensed victualler records Roger Hellier was named as either a victualler himself or as a guarantor for most years between 1771 and 1803. In the earlier years the names of the inns are not given, but we know that between 1788 and 1801 he was licensee of the King's Head, a pub which was demolished when the canal was built, and in 1802 and 1803 he was at the Hoop Inn, the whereabouts of which are not clear. Roger Hellier died and was buried in Sampford Peverell in 1810.

Apprentice Robert Mutter also appears in the parish records of the Overseers of the poor because he fathered Sarah Bidgood's illegitimate child, Robert Mutter Bidgood, who was born in October 1800. Robert was ordered to pay Sarah a sum of £1 10s 6d, and then 1s 6d every week.

Another tailor whose name appears in the apprenticeship and overseer accounts is William Hellyer, who may have been a relative of Roger Hellier (surname spellings varied). William Hellyer took on an apprentice, Thomas Ottway, in 1787 in his role as a tailor, but as we can see from the chapter on Grocers and Drapers he later became a stay-maker.

19th century tailors and the Taylor family

In the 19th century we can identify more tailors, thanks to the parish records and the censuses, and we start to hear about the tailoring Taylor family, starting in 1816 with the baptism in Sampford Peverell of Elizabeth Taylor, the daughter of Richard Taylor, a tailor, and his wife Mary. Next we have William Taylor who was born in Sampford Peverell in 1782. His father, also William Taylor, let's call him William Taylor 1, appeared regularly in the licensed victuallers lists as either a licensee or as a guarantor, usually at the Royal Oak in Higher Town (near where the school is now). We don't know if he was also a tailor but it is likely as he sometimes backs or is backed by Roger Hellier. His son 'William Taylor jnr' as he was at this time, let's call him William Taylor 2, also appears in these licensee lists from 1803 onwards. William Taylor 2 married Elizabeth Bidgood in 1802, and they had two children: Harriet and William (William Taylor 3). At the time of the 1841 census he was living in Higher Town with his second wife, Mary, and a journeyman tailor, Richard Hurford, was living with them. William Taylor 2 was a parish constable (this was a part-time role additional to a man's main job) from 1844 to 1855[43], and the account of a case in which he was involved in 1845, along with another tailor, James Clist, gives an example of a tailor being asked to convert an old garment. A young man was accused of stealing a coat from the house of John Bidgood in Willand. The newspaper report[36] of the trial describes James Clist, a tailor of Sampford Peverell, giving evidence to the effect that

> *'On the 6th June, prisoner brought me a coat and asked me to make it into a jacket* [presumably to disguise it], *which I promised to do. On the following Wednesday Taylor, the constable,* [who had apprehended the culprit] *came to me, and I gave him the coat, which was identified by prosecutor* [Bidgood]'.

William Taylor's signature (i.e. William 2) on 1852 petition   Courtesy of findmypast.co.uk

Peter Kerslake's signature on 1852 petition Courtesy of findmypast.co.uk

By 1851 William Taylor 2 had moved down to Lower Town, and the 1850 trade directory describes him both as a tailor and as running the Post Office, probably in part of Challis House, near the Globe. His son William Taylor 3, also a tailor, and William 3's son John Taylor, another tailor, both lived in Higher Town. Other tailors in the 1840s and 1850s were Thomas Hosegood, a constable in 1844 who later moved to Halberton, and James Clist and Peter Kerslake who both lived in Higher Town. William Taylor 3 was also a constable, like his father, serving from 1845 until 1872.

The 1861 village tailors included the three generations of Taylors (William 2 in the Lower Town Post Office, and William 3 and his son John in Higher Town), John Acland in Higher Town, and Joseph Goffin in Boobery. Joseph Goffin, born in about 1825, was the son of a Sampford Peverell carpenter, Thomas Goffin. In 1851 he was a journeyman tailor in Bristol, apparently with a wife named Sarah, but by 1855 he was back in Sampford Peverell, still as a tailor, but declaring himself to be a bachelor and marrying his cousin, Jane Goffin. They went on to have three children, but sadly his two little girls, aged 4 and 8, died within a few months of each other in 1864, in the scarlet fever epidemic which killed many youngsters in the village in that year. His son Thomas survived and lived to the age of 90. Initially the Goffins lived in Boobery, but by 1870 Joseph had taken over the licence of the New Inn in Higher Town, although he continued to work as a tailor, carrying on both businesses until the 1890s. In 1871 he was joined at the New Inn by his nephew, Thomas Ponsford, also a tailor. The

Joseph Goffin's signature on 1852 petition

census that year adds another generation to the Taylor family: William 2 had died in December 1861 but William 3 and his son John were still tailors and were joined in the business by John's son Thomas.

In February 1865 John Taylor was assaulted[37]. The account of the case is interesting in that it shows that tailors sometimes carried cloth and pattern books with them. John Taylor had gone to Westleigh to take a waistcoat to Robert Trevellian, "which event they celebrated by going to Fry's public house." When they left they met two young men who said that Taylor was drunk so, for his own safety, as he said he was going to walk back to Sampford along the canal, they locked him in a linhay for half an hour and then took him to the local constable. John Taylor said it was the two men who were drunk, and that they knocked him down, pulled him about in the mud, tore his coat and thrust him in a stable. Then they took him to the constable's house, knocked a bundle of cloth from under his arm, and threw his two pattern books about the road. Robert Trevellian said Taylor was not drunk: "they drank three quarts of cider together, but were a long time discussing it," and he testified to the brutal behaviour of the defendants. John Taylor's father, William, said Taylor was confined to bed for two days afterwards and had a bruise on his back. The bench decided that the accused were guilty of assault – they were convicted and each fined 50s or a month's imprisonment.

Tailors often had cash flow problems; they had to balance the payments they had to make for cloth, against the income they expected from the garments they sold. In February 1866 Joseph Goffin brought a court case against John Cottrell "for £1 5s 6d, money lent. Ordered to pay 3s a month."[38] A few months later William Taylor was ordered to repay 16s 8d, money he owed to F R Hodge, a draper

The tailor Child Land by Pietsch and Rictor on www.gutenberg.org

142

from Barnstaple who was suing a number of people for non-payment of goods supplied.[39]

The only tailors listed in the trade directories in the 1860s were William and John Taylor and Joseph Goffin, so it is likely that other tailors in the village at the time, such as John Seldon and Edwin Vickery who both lived in Higher Town, did not run their own businesses. Edwin Vickery, born in 1846, the son of local blacksmith Thomas Vickery, also appeared in the directories from 1878 onwards. He married Sarah Ann Wood, daughter of the harness maker Henry Wood, on 17th July 1872, by which time he was already qualified as a tailor. They had a long marriage but did not have any children.

In 1879 John Seldon, who lived in Canal Cottages, on Turnpike, was fined for not sending his child to school - he had only attended on 33 days out of 94. It seems pay was not good for a jobbing tailor. The boy's mother appeared in court and said "her husband was a tailor and had only half work, for which he got 6s 6d weekly. She had six children, and four attended school besides the one complained of. She was not aware but that the lad was old enough to go only half time, and had done so."[40] The Bench said she must send the boy to school and she was fined 2s 6d.

In November 1880 Joseph Goffin placed an advertisement in the Western Times: "WANTED a good TAILOR; single man preferred. Apply to Mr GOFFIN, Tailor, Sampford Peverell."

The 1881 census lists six tailors in the village: Edwin Vickery, in Canal Cottages, Turnpike (next door to his father-in-law, Henry Wood),John Seldon, now in Cross Hill, Thomas Ponsford in Turnpike, John Goffin at the New Inn, William Taylor 3 whose home and/or shop was next to London House in Higher Town, and John Taylor who was next door to Cowlins (now 14, Higher Town), but young Thomas Taylor had moved to Tiverton to live with his uncle, and was working as a mason. Cowlins, the neighbouring premises to John Taylor's, was a grocer's and draper's shop, so it must have been convenient that the tailor's and draper's were next door to each other.

John Seldon and his family moved to South Wales, and William Taylor 3 died In 1889 but in 1891 there were still four tailors in Sampford: Joseph Goffin at the New Inn, his nephew Thomas Ponsford in Turnpike, Edwin Vickery in Turnpike Cottage, and John Taylor in Higher Town, near Cowlins.

There was a court case in 1894 involving Thomas Ponsford and Frank Taylor, one of the sons of John Taylor, the tailor[41]. Frank was working for a miller in Halberton when he and Robert Bater, a carter, both of Halberton, were summoned for "having stolen between the 4th and 6th January two and a half sacks of barley meal of the value of £1 8s 9d, the property of Richard Westcott, miller and farmer, Nether Mills, Halberton. Thomas Ponsford, tailor, Sampford Peverell, was summoned for receiving the same knowing the meal to have been stolen." The miller had been suspicious for a while that he was being robbed, so "on January 6th he concealed himself on Mr Salter's premises at Sampford Peverell and saw Bater, the carter, stop at Ponsford's, which was opposite Salter's, and deliver barley meal." The Salter referred to here was Joseph Salter, a dairyman occupying Boobiers on the south side of Turnpike, and Thomas Ponsford lived on the north side of the road in Turnpike Cottage. The delivery was not recorded in the delivery book, and when police later checked Ponsford's premises they found three of the miller's sacks, though one was accounted for. The carter said he was now using a different book to record deliveries, because the miller had not given him a spare one when asked earlier. Doubt was thrown on whether the entries in the new book were genuine or were added later. Ponsford explained that he needed the meal as he kept several horses, pigs and poultry, and as a regular customer he was expecting to be billed for the meal in due course. The sacks of meal were delivered in daylight and were kept in a shed at the back of Ponsford's, which was not locked, so there was no attempt at concealment. Various witnesses, including William 'Cocky' Dunn the shoemaker, came forward to attest to the good character of the accused, especially Frank Taylor. The magistrates took a long time to consider the case and decided to give the defendants the benefit of the doubt. In later years Thomas Ponsford gave up tailoring and concentrated on providing livery or stable facilities and he was also a fly or cab proprietor, a fly being a light carriage drawn by a single horse.

Another man to combine the roles of tailor and innkeeper was George Pinson. Three daughters were born to him and his wife Hannah in the late 1890s, and at their baptisms he was described as a tailor and innkeeper. He was the licensee of the Globe, but had left it by 1901[7], when the tailors in the village were Joseph Goffin, now retired, in Boobery, John Taylor in Higher Town, Thomas Ponsford in Turnpike, and Edwin Vickery who was sharing Wharf Cottage with his in-laws.

20th century tailors

Joseph Goffin died in 1903, John Taylor died in 1908, and Thomas Ponsford gave up tailoring, so by 1911 there was just one tailor in Sampford: Edwin Vickery, in Wharf Cottage (now number 4), Turnpike. His in-laws were now living next door in Rose Cottage. In 1910 Wharf Cottage was a cob and slate house with a passage, parlour and kitchen downstairs and two bedrooms upstairs[2]. He continued to work as a tailor until at least 1926[42] and died, aged 83, in 1929, two years after Frank Kingdom, an experienced tailor from Halberton, moved to Sampford Peverell, perhaps to take over Edwin Vickery's work.

Frank Kingdom set up his tailor's business in Cowlins, 14, Higher Town, and there is much more about him and his shop in the chapter on Grocers and Drapers. He moved to Sampford from Halberton, and came from a family of tailors. His daughter Joan told us that her grandfather and uncles referred to their position as tailors as being 'On the Board'. Joan believed that this came from the fact that tailors did actually sit cross-legged on a board, as did Frank Kingdom. A website which lists tailoring terms has something similar - it includes the phrase "have you been on the board?" as meaning "are you experienced?"

'Tailor' Kingdom, as Frank was known, was described as a Master Tailor in the 1939 Register. He made suits and breeches, commonly worn by farmers, and was always very busy. Working by the light of the window Frank would sit in the traditional cross-legged position, where he was often seen by boys from the St Boniface Home. For a bit of fun he would drop his false teeth out, and the Home boys would run away! He made and sold clothes in his Higher Town shop for over thirty years, until his retirement in 1965, which brought to an end the long history of tailoring in Sampford Peverell.

Frank Kingdom 'on the board'   *Illustration by Gerald Dinnage*

Chapter 9

Shops in 2020

Little Turberfield Farm Shop – Station Road

This business began in 1980. Eric Cole acquired his knowledge of the butchery trade working for his father Lionel at "Page's Butchers" in Bampton Street, Tiverton in the 1960s and 1970s. He married Julie Passmore in 1967 and in 1980 they purchased Little Turberfield Farm in Station Road, Sampford Peverell. Previously owned by Lawrence Disney, the property consisted of a farm house, outbuildings and 77 acres, but Eric and Julie soon found the area too large to manage and sold 30 acres to a neighbouring farmer.

They raised cattle, sheep, chickens and turkeys, and grew their own vegetables... and also strawberries, one of the local outlets for which was the Hartnoll Hotel in Tiverton; one of their guests was so impressed with the quality and flavour of the fruit served to him for dessert one evening that he asked where they came from. This resulted in a gentleman turning

up at the Farm Shop asking to buy some strawberries, at which point Eric gave him a basket and pointed to the field, indicating that the man, who spoke with an American accent, should pick his own. That man was none other than the famous film actor Cary Grant!

Eric had begun selling his produce 'at the farm gate' but in November 1985 he opened his shop in a

Farm shop, 1980s

147

converted cow shippen beside the farmhouse. In those days no planning permission was required for a 'Farm Shop' provided it sold only home grown produce and nothing was bought in. He took £30 on his first day of business and finished the week with a grand total of £320. He was a man ahead of his time and tried to be as 'organic' as possible before organic farming was commonplace. All the animal feed for his stock came from a feed mill in Halberton, and he particularly requested that no antibiotics or growth promoters should be added. None of his sausages (which he made himself at the shop) contained preservatives and they were seasoned only with salt and pepper. He also catered for people with food intolerances.

With the demise of very local abattoirs Eric had his animals slaughtered at Lloyd Maunders in Willand until a supermarket chain insisted that they must specialise in lamb, and he transferred to Stillman's in Taunton. Chickens were prepared on the premises, just a couple at a time, and sometimes when the stock of vegetables ran out in the shop Julie would have to run up to the acre of ground on which they grew beans and sprouts etc. and pick what the customer wanted while they waited. By 1990 the business was so good that Eric and Julie employed 4 staff members and also took on another butcher by the name of Richard Burton (not, on this occasion, a well-known actor!)

In the early 1990s Mid Devon District Council conducted a survey of local amenities and suggested that the district around Sampford Peverell would benefit from a running track and a golf driving range. As Eric was a keen golfer he applied to develop land on the opposite side of the road from the shop as a Driving Range; his application was successful and by 1994 the enterprise was up and running. By 1995 the Farm Shop business had expanded to the point where the converted cowshed was no longer adequate, but Eric's application to build larger premises on land adjacent to the Driving Range (although supported by the Parish Council) was refused by Mid Devon District Council. The Coles decided to sell the farmhouse, outbuildings and 7 acres of land to Geoff Persey but kept 20 acres of grass keep, in addition to the Driving Range which was leased to Stuart Sawyer, who later expanded it to an 18 acre 9 hole Golf Course. The athletically-inclined of Sampford Peverell are still waiting for their running-track!

On vacating the farmhouse, Eric and Julie moved to Tiverton but leased the shop premises back from Geoff Persey for a further 5 years, during which time they took on Sue Clifford-Parry, who had been working for Huggett's Butchers of Silverton. Finally in 2000 the Coles felt ready to retire and offered the business to Sue, on the understanding that she bought all the stock and equipment. This she did, paying a monthly sum until the purchase was complete.

Little Turberfield Farm Shop continued in business, being well supported by local customers and many from further afield, as well as supplying Devon "Red Ruby" beef to outlets as far away as London. All Sue's employees lived locally and between them they maintained the good reputation which the Cole family had built up. They survived a severe rainstorm in 2012 which flooded the shop and disabled the refrigerated display cabinets; however, the meat storage room was not affected and, thanks to the concerted efforts of the staff, they were able to continue trading.

In 2011 Sue, who up to this point had advertised only locally, decided to spread the Little Turberfield name more widely and took a full page in the "Guide to Rural England – Devon", an up-market publication by Travel Publishing Ltd (no longer in existence). There were two colour photographs and a comprehensive description of the shop and the goods on offer, e.g.:

> Little Turberfield Farm Shop can be found in the lovely mid-Devon village of Sampford Peverell. ...it stocks a wide range of some of the best locally-produced foods...free-range meat, home-made sausages and burgers, a choice of items for the summer barbecue, and plenty

The Farm shop, 2018   *Photo: Peter Bowers*

of home-baked pies and pasties. Real Devon ice cream...can be found here, and there's a good choice of fruit and vegetables, and local and international cheeses. Local jams and home-made bread can also be found in the shop, which is full of old-world charm with its attractive beamed ceilings

There is no record, of course, of how much extra business this advertising created, but clearly things were getting difficult and in February 2015 Sue closed the Farm Shop without warning and left the village. The premises remained closed for several months and it was feared that the residents of Sampford Peverell, who had enjoyed the convenience and pleasure of having a local farm shop for some 35 years, would again have to travel further afield for their fresh meat, eggs and vegetables. However, all was not lost, and on 1st July 2015 Little Turberfield Farm Shop reopened under the new management of experienced husband-and-wife team Graham and Beverley Sanders. This is how they describe their enterprise:

> Traditional farm shop full of local produce. In house butchery with local longhorn beef, lamb, pork, poultry and Christmas turkeys. Plus cheese, fruit and vegetables, preserves, bakery, dairy. Everything you need for your weekly food shop with service to match.

You can even get a cup of coffee there now, and the business is currently well-supported by Sampford Peverell residents.

SPAR shop, 3a The Mews, Smithys Way

There used to be a garage (Kelland's) with a shop in Lower Town which closed in the early 2000s. The site was cleared and left for some years before it was eventually re-developed as housing. One of the planning conditions for the development, to be called Smithys Way, was that it had to include a shop. When the developer, Cavannah Homes, completed the works in 2008, the village was provided with a new shop - the only one in Lower Town. It was taken on from the beginning by Paul Goddard and his partner Becky, who established it under the retail chain and franchise brand of SPAR.

Being sited next to the main road through the village, it soon attracted passing trade as well as becoming popular with the residents. After the Post Office in Higher Town closed in January 2010, further opportunities were opened up for expansion. The SPAR shop was now the only retailer of basic groceries and newspapers in the village, and Paul and Becky saw a rapid growth in custom from local residents. The loss of the facility of the

Post Office was also addressed when the provision of postal services was incorporated into the SPAR shop in 2011.

In 2019 the Spar shop continues as the village Post Office and sells an enormous variety of goods: newspapers, periodicals, greetings cards and groceries, including fruit, vegetables, dairy produce, ice cream, tobacco products, alcohol, sweets, takeaway snacks and coffee plus a variety of lottery cards. The notice board is well used, keeping customers informed about what's going on in the village, and the shop also stocks copies of the cards and books produced by the Sampford Peverell Society!

The Spar shop, 2018   *Photo: Peter Bowers*

Notes

[1] An unusual term, believed to mean 'second mortgage'

[2] The 1910-1915 land valuation and ownership survey was undertaken for taxation purposes. It is sometimes referred to as the Lloyd George survey. The field books contain details of every property in the country. There are four field books which cover Sampford Peverell, and they are held in the National Archives. The details include owners, occupiers, numbers of rooms, outbuildings, and occasionally hand-drawn plans of farms.

[3] 1851 census

[4] Kelly's directory 1856

[5] Trade directories and 1881 census

[6] The 1939 Register was compiled as the result of the National Registration Act in September 1939. Enumerators visited every household in Britain, gathering names, addresses, birth dates, occupations and so on. This information was used to issue identity cards. The data can be searched in www.findmypast.co.uk

[7] 1901 census

[8] Land tax returns

[9] Kelly's directory 1856

[10] Exeter and Plymouth Gazette 30 November 1860

[11] Tiverton Gazette 29 January 1861

[12] Western Times, 14 June 1862

[13] Western Times, 9 November 1866

[14] 1881 census

[15] Exeter and Plymouth Gazette 6 February 1886, quoting the London Gazette.

[16] Exeter and Plymouth Gazette 24 November 1894

[17] 1861 census

[18] Western Times 12 March 1888

[19] Western Times 8 March 1901

[20] Western Times 19 April 1921

[21] A lease could last a number of years or until certain named people, such as those living in the property, had died.

[22] History and Mystery in Sampford Peverell, Roger Thorne, 1993.

[23] The Gentleman's Magazine and Historical Chronicle Volume 78 part 1

[24] Green Shield stamps were stamps which shoppers could collect and then use, when they had enough, to buy items from a catalogue

[25] 1881 census

[26] Electoral rolls

[27] 1844 Tithe appointment

[28] Early 19th Century rate books for Sampford Peverell

[29] North Devon Journal 14 April 1831

[30] School log book

[31] 1841 census

[32] We think this must mean the Tiverton edition of the Western Times.

[33] A Postal Order is similar to a cheque but it is something you can buy in a Post Office without having a bank account, to send to someone by post as payment or as a gift.

[34] Kelly's Directory 1873

[35] See Cluett, D. and Sampford Peverell Society, *A village childhood..*in the Bibliography

[36] Western Times, 26 July 1845

[37] Western Times 14 February 1865 and Exeter Flying Post 15 February 1865

[38] Western Times 6 February 1866

[39] Tiverton Gazette 5 June 1866

[40] Schools and local authorities had different regulations and some allowed older children to go part-time if they were needed to help at home or go to work to earn money.

[41] Western Times 17 January 1894

[42] Kelly's directory 1926

[43] List of constables on www.sampevsoc.co.uk/occupation-records.html

Appendix 1

The 1852 Petition

In 1852 a petition was signed by 49 Sampford Peverell tradesmen asking for a free pardon for a young man named Richard Parker who was one of two men convicted and sentenced to transportation for raping 15-year-old Emma Coles, the daughter of the landlord of the New Inn. Parker said he was innocent, was said to be of good character and was depended on by his widowed mother. The other man convicted, John Elworthy, had admitted to the crime and said that Parker was not involved. The petition was successful and surprisingly both young men were granted a free pardon, though Elworthy did not return to the village. We do not know what happened to the poor girl.

Transcript of the names of the Sampford Peverell tradesmen who signed the petition

Francis Frederick Taylor *Solicitor*
John Bennett *Baker*
William Adams *Engineer*
Samuel Lawrence *Schoolmaster*
George Burridge *Hop Merchant*
Richard Jennings *Painter etc*
John Goffin *Builder*
Thomas Kerslake *Lime Burner*
John Kerslake *Lime Burner*
James Stevens *Lime Burner*
Francis Hellier *Gardener*
George Goffin *Carpenter*
Richard Darch *Cordwainer*
George Saunders *Mason*
William Harris *Carpenter*
Thomas Payne *Youman (sic)*
Joseph Goffin *Taylor*
John Darch *Boot & Shoe maker*
William Curwood *Mason*
John Greenslade *Butcher*
Robert Kerslake *Yeoman*
Davis Parr *Basket Maker*
John Pugsley *Farryer (sic)*
Benjiman Calbreath *Coopper (sic)*
Peter Kerslake *Tailor*

James Farr *Wheelwright*
Thomas Farr *Carpenter*
Richard Harris *Draper etc*
Richard Southwood *Baker*
John Fisher *Yeoman*
Richard Webber *Yeoman*
Jno. Rd. Chave *Schoolmaster*
George Hellyer *Draper*
Thos. Southwood *Baker etc*
Mark Saunders *Builder*
James Vickery *Blacksmith*
James Mutter *Mason*
Thomas Payne *Yeoman*
Joseph Creed *Millwright*
John Goffin *Carpenter*
Tho. Bowden *Yeoman*
William Taylor Snr *Tailor*
Peter Arthurs *Smith*
Francis Needs *Shoemaker*
Levi Saunders *Baker*
Thomas Goffin *Innkeeper*
William Shackell *Butcher*
Thomas Vickery *Blacksmith*
David Parr *Thatcher*

Appendix 2

Examples of Mr Thomas's Advertisements

In the early years of the 1960s 'Red' Thomas placed advertisements in the Parish News every month for his grocer's shop, Challis Stores. At that time small grocery stores in rural villages were having to compete with rapidly-expanding supermarket businesses, situated in nearby towns. This selection of his advertisements shows the efforts that he made to ensure that his customers were made aware of the advantages of shopping locally - with him, of course!

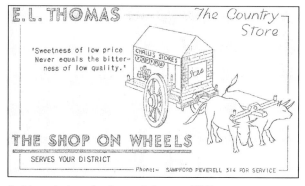

E. L. THOMAS ———— The Country Store

"Sweetness of low price Never equals the bitterness of low quality."

CHALLIS STORES

THE SHOP ON WHEELS

SERVES YOUR DISTRICT

Phone:- SAMPFORD PEVERELL 314 FOR SERVICE

Parish magazine advertisement, January 1957

> Out on a country round one of our very aged customers went into one of these new-fangled shops to get some chocolate and biscuits and "Do you know Mr Thomas, I stood there an hour and nobody came to serve me, and they lost no end of stuff because I saw several people popping things into their shopping bags. I walked out in disgust." I didn't have the heart to tell her she was in a self-service store.

Parish magazine advertisement (extract), June 1961

Parish magazine advertisement, March 1960

"Hullo, so you shop here too".

"Yes, I used to think I saved money by going to Tiverton but Mr. Thomas stocks everything here and his special offers are as cheap as anywhere – it saves me two bus fares a week as well."

"Do you know about his Saving Club? – It's amazing – you get 2/6 in the £ that's 12½% interest – 12½%! more than anywhere else."

"You're right and that's not all – in Tiverton the Christmas Club must all be spent in the shop but here Mr. Thomas'll give you cash. Of course people take advantage of him, but I'm going to buy all I can from him. If he treats us well we should give him a fair deal."

"By the way, does your mother know of the travelling shop? My mother finds she can buy all she wants from it and says nothing is ever too much trouble."

"Thanks, I'll tell mother to look out for it, I must run now but we'll meet here often. Everyone says, go to Thomas's if you want to meet your friends 'Bye."

YOUR COUNTRY GROCER

Orders delivered daily

Phone: 314

E. L. THOMAS

Parish magazine advertisement, August 1960

158

Sources

Devon Heritage Centre
Sampford Peverell Primary School
Somerset Heritage Centre
The National Archives
Tiverton Museum of Mid Devon Life
www.ancestry.co.uk
www.artic.edu/collection
www.britishnewspaperarchives.co.uk

www.findmypast.co.uk
www.gutenberg.org
www.sampevsoc.co.uk
www.specialcollections.le.ac.uk
www.victorianweb.org

Bibliography

1. Bond, C. and Sampford Peverell Society, *The schools of Sampford Peverell : two centuries of education*. 2015, Sampford Peverell: Sampford Peverell Society. .

2. Brown, T., *Devon Ghosts*. 1982; Jarold & Sons.

3. Cluett, D. and Sampford Peverell Society, *A village childhood : memories of living in rural Devon before the age of the motor car*. Sampford Peverell Society publication. 2007, Great Britain: Charles Scott-Fox.

4. Mingay, G.E., *The Victorian countryside*. 1981, London: Routledge & Kegan Paul.

5. Pinchbeck, I., *Women Workers and the Industrial Revolution, 1750-1850*. Routledge, 2004

6. Scott-Fox, C., *Sampford Peverell : the village, church, chapels and rectories : from saxon 'vill' to 20th century village; the history of Sampford Peverell and its ecclesiastical buildings*. 2007, England: Charles Scott-Fox.

7. Shammas, C., *The Pre-Industrial Consumer in England and America*. 1990, Oxford: Clarendon. Especially chapter 8, 'Rise of the English Country Shop'.

8. Wyatt, P., *The Uffculme Wills and Inventories: 16th to 18th Centuries*. 1997 , Devon and Cornwall Record Society Publications.

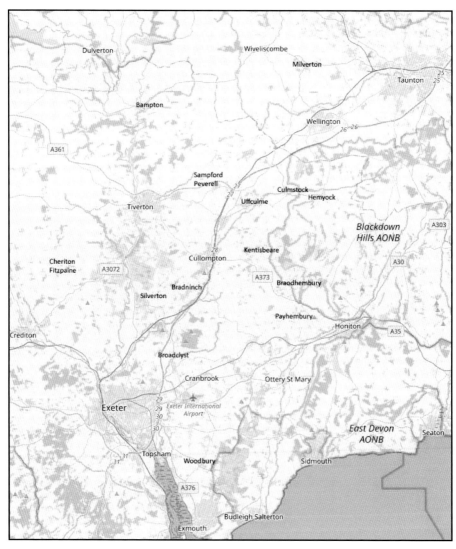

Map showing Sampford Peverell in the Greater Exeter area
©OpenStreetMap contributors openstreetmap.org/copyright

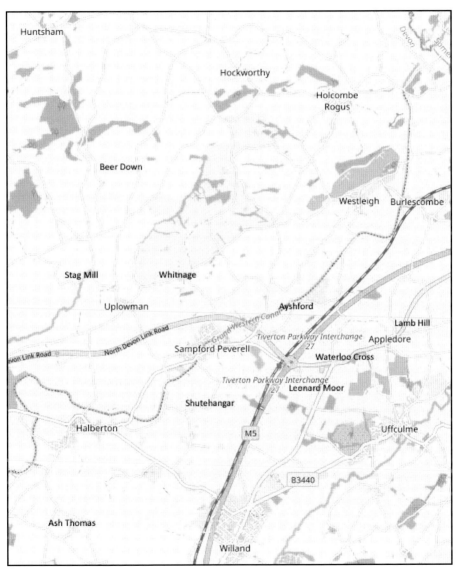

Map showing Sampford Peverell and surrounding villages and hamlets
©OpenStreetMap contributors openstreetmap.org/copyright

Map showing Sampford Peverell streets and landmarks in 2020.
©OpenStreetMap contributors openstreetmap.org/copyright

Index of surnames and property names

All properties in Sampford Peverell, unless shown otherwise

Acland — 141
Adcock — 19
Alford — 58, 59, 82
Always Cottage — 135
Avery — 72, 118, 133

Bailey — 134
Baker — 76
Bale — 139
Ball — 132
Ballamy — 7, 10, 15
Ballamys (Ballamy's) — 11, 51
Banfild (Banfield) — 10
Barum House — **76-87, 102-103, 104-105**
Baskerville — 89
Bater — 143, 144
Beaufort — 5
Beavis — 48
Beedell — 29
Bennett — **23-25**
Bible Christian Chapel — 69, 74
Bidgood — 28, 140, 141
Bidgoods — 47
Billinghay — 137
Blackaller (Blakaller) — 56, 125
Blackmore — 136
Blake — 18, 79
Boobery Cottage — 46
Boobery, nos 8 and 10 see Drakes & Rows
Boobiers — 144
Bowbeer — 63
Bowbeere — 126
Bowden — 30, 41, 43
Bower — 125
Bowerman — 38
Bray — 30
Brice — 125
Bridge House — 72, 95, 101, **110-112, 114-115**
Bright — 35
Broom — 134, 136

Buckingham — 95
Bucknell — 95
Bult — 42
Burlescombe, Horse & Jockey — 47
Burman — 138
Burrough — 70
Burroughs — 12
Burton — 148
Bussel, van — 74, 120
Bussell — 18
Butteridge — 42

Calbraith — 24
Canal Cottages — 143
Canal Grounds — 42
Canningtons & Rows — 42
Capron — 136
Carpenter — 68
Carter — 13
Chains Cottage — 135
Chains Road, no 6 — **23-25**
Challis — **28-37**,40-42, 47, 48, **88-89**, 92, 108, 109
Challis Cottage (Challis Stores, Salter's Stores, Sampford Stores, The Handy Shop) — 28, 80, 84, **88-100, 115-116, 156-158**
Challis House — 28, 43, 84, **88-100, 108-110**, 141
Challis Stores — see Challis Cottage
Chamberlain — 104
Channon — 80
Chapman — 4
Chappell — 71
Chave — 11, 12, 23, 28
Cherry — 98
Chidgey — 22, 65
Chorleys — 22, 25, 38, **50-56**, 60
Church — 36, 82, 86
Clark — 126
Clarke — 7
Clifford-Parry — 148-150

Clist	140, 141	Elston	32
Cluett	14, 39, 40, 57, 78, 79,	Elworthy	47, 126, 127, 134, 155
	93, 102, 113, 130	Evans	27, 65
Cole	49, 147-149	Exeter, Gaol	52
Coles	**25**	Exeter, Holloway Street, Home of the	
Collins	11-13, 20, 21	Good Shepherd	114
Coombe Cottage	**74-75**, 135, 136	Exeter, Lion's Halt	13
Cork	67	Exeter, St Mary Major	50
Cornall	38		
Cornish	67, 103, 113, 114, 136	Farr	28, 114
Coronation Cottages	45, 95, 110,	Farrs	42
	116, 117, 136	Ferguson	72, 118
Cory	66	Fewings	47
Coteyle de	2	Fisher	30, **43-44**
Cottey	24	Flatters	72-74, 105, 119, 120,133
Cottrell	142	Fowler	30
Court	58	Francis	57, 76
Cowling	7	Frost	75
Cowlins	**60-68**, 143, 145	Fry	57
Creamery, The	see *Norrish's Creamery*	Fullers	139
Creed	90		
Cross Hill	50, 54, 127,	Gabbey	85-87, 105
	129, 138, 139, 143,	Gee	84, 85, 105
Crosse	56	Ghost House, The	**10-19**, 20, 21,
Croydon	139		42, 51, 52
Curram Meadow	42	Gibbins (Gibbons)	133
Curwood	7, 8, 69, 125, 137	Gillard	13
		Glanville	46
Daniel	74, 75	Globe Cottage	30
Darch	51, 101, **126-129**, 134	Globe Inn	29, 30, 42, 43,
Davey	77		108, 109, 116, 141, 144
Davis	41	Goddard	150
Dawbney	28	Goffin	32, 47, 55, 67, 72,
Dillon	47		95, 114, 115, 141-144
Dinham	64, 65	Grant	18, 19, 140, 147
Disney	147	Greaves	128
Downie	45	Green Headlands	68
Drake	138, 139	Greenslade	**42**
Drakes and Rows	138	Gunn	30, 92
Drewe	28	Guppy	35
Druller	134	Gwinell	82
Dunn	31, 57, 58, 66, 126,		
	129-130, 136, 144	Haddon	44
Dynham	4	Halberton, Battens Cottage	37
		Halberton, Hill Head	65
East Devon County School	12, 24, 110	Halberton, Nether Mills	144

Halberton, Swan Inn 131
Hall 27
Halls (Halls Cottage, Halls House, Higher
Town Stores) **56-60**, 67, 76,
104, 109, 129, 130, 136
Handy Shop, The *see Challis Cottage*
Hare and Hounds 31, 45, 134, 136
Harris 69, 70, 129, 134
Harwood 60
Hawkins 103
Hellier (Hellyer) 7, 50-54,
60-63, 70, 71, 140

Hemyock, Bubhays 43
Herford 82
Heritage Meadow 51
Hewett 108
Heywood 12
High Cross House 134
Higher Town Stores *see Halls*
Higher Town, no 4 11, **20-22**, 25
Higher Town, no 9 *see Chorleys*
and Paulett House
Higher Town, no 11 *see Rose Cottage*
Higher Town, no 11a *see Halls*
Higher Town, no 14 **22**, 53, 54,
and see Cowlins
Higher Town, no 17 15, 18
Higher Town, no 18 *see Ghost House, The*
Higher Town, no 21 *see London House*
Higher Town, no 24 *see Coombe Cottage*
Higher Town, no 32 35
Hill 21
Hill Kiln 63, 107
Hirschfeld 35, 36
Hodder 22
Hodge 142
Holland 84
Hollands Stores *see Barum House*
Holley 66, 83, 97
Holloway 22, 63-66
Holway 20
Hookway 82
Hoop Inn 140
Hooper **47-48**
Hosegood 141
Howe 104

Hukely 56
Hurford 126, 140
Hussey 133

Ingersent 54
Isaac 37, 50

Jacobs 24, **44-45**
Jennings 57, 72, 76-80, 90,
101-103, 108-112, 117
Jutson (Jutsum) 28, 138, 139

Karslake 77
Kelland's Garage 105, 150
Kemp 32
Kerslake 28, 62, 63, 80, 141
Kerslakes 42
Key Head *see Quay Head*
Kiln House 63
King 28, 74
Kingdom 66-68, 104, 145
Kings (Kings Cottage,
Kings Cottages) 45, 47, 110
King's Head 140
Knight 14, 53, 54, 63, 71
Knowles 25, 58, 82-84, 105

Lamb 37
Lamb Hill 83
Land 126
Langham 28
Lanyon 92
Leach 136
Leary 72, 119, 120
Lee 79
Little Garth Cottage 35
Little Shambles 27
Little Turberfield Farm
(Little Turberfield Farm Shop) **48, 147-150**
Lock 23
London House (London Inn)
15, 67, **69-74**, 101, **105-106**, **112-114**,
117-120, 129, 132, 133, 136, 143
Lovell 21, 76, 135
Lower Town, no 2 *see Bridge House*

Lower Town, nos 8, 10 and 12 *see Challis, Challis Cottage and Challis House*

Lower Town, nos 25 and 27 *see Barum House*

Luxon 12, 13

Manley 28, 41
Mann 99
Manners 111
Marble Arch 14
Mariansleigh, Butcher's Arms 46
Marley 34
Marsh 28, 138
Martin 69
Maynard 15-19, 67
Melhuish 60, 125
Merriemeade 23, 84
Methodist Chapel 16, 51, 110, 130
Metton 4
Middleton 35
Mill Cottage 18
Milton 14
Mitchell's 139
Moor End House (Moorend) 34, 133
Moor plot & Moor Meadows 42
Morgan 30, 45, 70, 71, 136
Morles 42
Morrell 103, 104
Morrells Farm (Morrell's Farm) 43, 46, 89
Mountain Oak *see Mount Stephen Oak*
Mount Pleasant **25**, 111
Mount Stephen Oak (Mount Stephen, Mountain Oak) 32, 43, 44
Moysey 111
Mutter 127, 140
Muzyka 68

Needes 47
Needs 134-136
Newcombe 31-34, 37, 41
New Inn 25, 47, 55, 68, 141, 143, 155
Nichols 57
Norrish 28, 64
Norrish's Creamery 23, 25, 64, 80
Northam 31
Old Barn 127

Ottway 140

Parker 21, 24, 128, 131, 155
Parkhouse 57, 72, 112, 117, **131-133**, 136
Parr 25, 54, 71, 108-110
Parsons 60, 68, 118, 119
Passmore 147
Paulett 2
Paulett House 25, **37-41**, 56
Pengelly 36, 82
Perkins 11
Perram 29
Perry 12, 86
Persey 148
Peverell 1, 2
Pine 29, 41, 42
Pinson 144
Podbury 135
Pond Cottage 46
Ponsford (Pounsford, Poundsfield) 30, 43, 89, 90, 112, 113, 131, 141, 143, 144
Poole 28, 138
Popham 41
Pounsford (Poundsfield) *see Ponsford*
Preece 71
Prickman 42, 140
Pringle 27
Providence House 30
Pullen 6, 7
Pyle 54

Quant 23
Quay Head (Key Head) 20, **37-41**
Quick 31, 89, 95

Radford 42, 95
Redstone 72, 117, 118, 132, 133
Reid 58, 81, 104
Rich 131
Richards 112
Riche 4, 5
Robertson 129, 135
Rolestone **46-47**, 135
Rose Cottage, Higher Town 50, 54, **103-104**
Rose Cottage, Turnpike 145

Rossiter 71, 72
Rowe 28, 37, 57
Royal Oak
(Royal Oak Cottages) 51-53, 61, 66, 140
Russell 39
Ryder 21, 22

Salter 37-41, 47, 56, 97, 144
Salter's Stores *see Challis Cottage*
Sampford Barton 14, 28, 46, 67
Sampford Mill 90
Sampford Peverell Halt 104
Sampford Peverell Primary School
10, 60, 74, 84
Sampford Stores *see Challis Cottage*
Sanders 150
Sanford 126
Saunders 6, 23, 24, 42, 69, 70, 125, 135
Sawyer 148
Seldon 143
Selley 19
Shackell 29, 30, 41, 42
Shallis 29, 88, 89
Shannon 95
Sharland 82
Shebbear, Lake Farm 74
Sheppards House 23
Sherry 70
Shuckburgh 7, 8, 42
Shutehangar Farm 37
Silverton, Huggett's Butchers 148
Simmons 82
Singer 125
Skinner 7, 94
Skinners 20-22, 55, 56
Slee's Morells 42
Smithy's Way, no 3a The Mews
see Spar shop
Smyth 4
Smyths 28
Snell 58, 99, 104
Snook 60
Snow 71, 133
Somerset, Street, Clarks' factory 125
Southwood **20-22**, 25, 38,
55, 56, 62, 71, 127

Spar shop 74, **106, 120-121, 150-151**
Spark 140
Sparkes 20
Spridell 97
Spring 94, 95, 97
St Boniface Home 18, 145
St John the Baptist Church 50, 60, 74
Station Road, Little Turberfield Farm Shop
see Little Turberfield Farm (Shop)
Stephens 55
Stevens 52, 91, 135
Stone 6, 7
Strong 108
Surridge 7, **42**
Sweetman 85, 105

Tally 10, 11
Tapper 76
Taudevin 91-94, 109
Taunton, Hanbury & Cotching 71
Taunton, Stillman's 148
Taylor 22, **25**, 42, 54, 55, 61,
67, 72, 90, 108, 109, 112-114, **140-144**
Thomas 13-19, 24, 36, 67,
80, 95, 96, 115, 116, **156-158**
Thorne 71, 74, 75
Tiverton Junction [Station] 113
Tiverton Parkway [Station] 48, 104
Tiverton, Bampton Street, Page's Butchers
147
Tiverton, Bampton Street, Symons' Bakers
21
Tiverton, Grammar School 67
Tiverton, Hamley's Mill 16
Tiverton, Hartnoll Hotel 147
Tiverton, Heathcoat's factory 58, 80
Tiverton, Heathcoat School 68
Towell 135
Townsend Field 29
Tremlett 76
Trevelian (Trevellian, Trevelyan, Trevellyan)
99, 132, 138, 142
Trott 31
Turner 120
Turnpike Cottage 143, 144
Turnpike, no 4 *see Wharf Cottage*

Uffculme, George Inn 134
Uffculme, Gore House 32, 37
Uffculme, Masonic Lodge 87
Uffculme, Railway Hotel 45
Upcott 13
Upham 80-83, 103-105
Uplowman Primary School 84
Uplowman, Lands Mill 20
Uplowman, Stag Mill 17, 81
Upton 50

Venton 72
Vickery 62, 76, 134, 143-145

Wading 13
Walters 72
Ware's 51
Warren 69
Webber 13, 82, 126, 134, 140
Wensley **45-46**, 47
Westcott 144
Westleigh, Ebear 47
Westleigh, Fry's public house 142
Wharf Cottage 41, 144, 145
Wharf House 18, 95, 114
Wheeler 34-37, 41, 48
White 93
Wilcox 126
Willand School 84
Willand, Halfway House Inn 24, 44
Willand, Lloyd Maunders 148
Williams 30-34, 41, 47, 62, 82
Wilson 83
Wine 27
Wood 12, 13, 18, 20, 29, 31, 135, 143
Worth Orchard 42
Wright 31, 59, 60, 65, 84, 98, 99
Wright & Sharland 19
Wynhay 4

Young 97, 98